HOW TO
THINK LIKE AN
ABSOLUTE
GENIUS

Quarto is the authority on a wide range of topics.

Quarto educates, entertains and enriches the lives of our readers—enthusiasts and lovers of hands-on living.

www.quartoknows.com

Graphic design: Isabelle Dumontaux
UK Editor: Harriet Stone

© 2018 Quarto Publishing plc
© Casterman - First French edition

First English edition published in 2018 by QEB Publishing,
an imprint of The Quarto Group.
6 Orchard Road, Suite 100
Lake Forest, CA 92630
T: +1 949 380 7510
F: +1 949 380 7575
www.QuartoKnows.com

A CIP record for this book is available from the Library of Congress.

ISBN 978 0 71123 985 2

Manufactured in Guangdong, China CC082018

9 8 7 6 5 4 3 2 1

Photo credits (t: top – r: right – l: left – c: center – b: bottom)

p.19bl, Hulton Archive/Getty Images; p.28t Salvador Dalí, The Persistence of Memory, 1931, Museum of Modern Art, New York, USA / © Salvador Dali, Fundació Gala-Salvador Dalí, DACS 2018; p.28bl Salvador Dalí, Sleep, c.1937, Private Collection /© Salvador Dali, Fundació Gala-Salvador Dalí, DACS 2018; p.28br Salvador Dalí, Slave Market with the Disappearing Bust of Voltaire, 1940, Salvador Dali Museum, St. Petersburg, Florida, USA / © Salvador Dali, Fundació Gala-Salvador Dalí, DACS 2018
p.28c Charles Hewitt / Stringer / Getty Images / © Salvador Dali, Fundació Gala-Salvador Dalí, DACS 2018; p.29cr Edvard Munch - The Scream, National Gallery, Oslo, Norway / classicpaintings / Alamy Stock Photo; p.43br Bettmann / Getty Images; p.46b Joan Miro - Untitled, 1938, Museum of Modern Art (MoMA), New York, USA / © Successió Miró / ADAGP, Paris and DACS London 2018; p.47c Pablo Picasso, Las Meninas, No.1, 1957, Museo Picasso, Barcelona, Spain / Bridgeman Images / © Succession Picasso/DACS, London 2018; p.47b Robert DOISNEAU / Gamma-Rapho/Getty Images / © Succession Picasso/ DACS, London 2018; p48-49 © ADAGP, Paris and DACS, London 2018; p.49cr Thomas Koehler / Photothek via Getty Images; p.52c Léon Spilliaert - Vertige, 1908, Royal Museums of Fine Arts of Belgium, Brussels; p.59t Rolls Press / Popperfoto/Getty Images; p.59cl Wikipedia; p.64c Bettmann / Getty Images; p.66c Marcel Duchamp, Fountain, 1917/64, The Israel Museum, Jerusalem, Bridgeman Images / © Association Marcel Duchamp / ADAGP, Paris and DACS, London 2018; p.66b Marcel Duchamp, The Bride Stripped Bare by Her Bachelors, Even (The Large Glass) 1915-23, Philadelphia Museum of Art, Pennsylvania, PA, USA / Bridgeman Images / © Association Marcel Duchamp / ADAGP, Paris and DACS, London 2018

All other images are Shutterstock or credited to the public domain.

Despite our best efforts, we were unable to reach certain rights holders. We invite them to contact us.

MIX
Paper from
responsible sources
FSC® C008047

HOW TO THINK LIKE AN ABSOLUTE GENIUS

Text and black and white illustrations:
Philippe Brasseur
Color illustrations : Virginie Berthemetv

CONTENTS

ARE WE ALL GENIUSES?

Are you smart enough to read this book?
Take this genius test to find out...

What is a genius?
A. A magical character who lives in a lamp
B. A person who is very intelligent and creative
C. In Roman times, a "genius" was a spirit connected to a person or place.

B and C. In modern times, the word "genius" means a person with an outstanding mind who has discovered or achieved something amazing.

Being a genius means being...
A. super-smart
B. super-hardworking

A and B. It's true that geniuses generally have an IQ well above average (140+). But this doesn't mean much on its own: intelligence leads to nothing without hard work. The world is full of hidden geniuses, i.e. very intelligent people who have never used their talent.

What do most geniuses have in common?
A. They were top of the class in school.
B. They often did badly in school.

B. Geniuses are scientists, writers, artists, and others who think beyond what is known and taught in school. Because of this, they are often considered stupid, as they don't fit the mold of school learning.

What field do geniuses work in?
A. The sciences
B. The arts
C. Any field

C. There are geniuses in the sciences and the arts, but also in cooking, sports, board games... anything and everything! What's your personal talent? Take the test on page 69 to find out!

Is being a genius really that great?
A. Abso-freakin'-lutely!
B. Meh...in some ways, but not in others.
C. It's atrocious, horrible, and diabolical!

B. Geniuses are often incredibly gifted in a certain subject... but not at all in others! For example, a mathematical genius might be unable to repair a plug, or a brilliant writer might struggle to hit a ball.

Genius is...
A. 10% inspiration and 90% perspiration
B. 50% inspiration and 50% perspiration
C. 90% inspiration and 10% perspiration

A. Many geniuses work hard from an early age to become "experts" in their field. By the age of 6, Mozart had already spent over 3,500 hours studying music with his father. The Polgar sisters were taken out of school by their father in order to train them as chess champions, and they have beaten many of the best players in the world.

Can I really become a genius like Einstein?
A. Yes, you just have to read this book!
B. Don't bother, you don't have the right genes.
C. Work to find what you are good at. Don't try to copy someone else.

C. Geniuses like Einstein and Picasso are unique and exceptional people, so there is no point trying to copy them. However, you can follow their example by becoming more creative and mentally "flexible"—letting the unique genius that lies within you burst forth!

AT A TRADITIONAL SCHOOL...

- It's <u>the teacher</u> who asks the questions (and they always know the answers).

- There is only <u>one</u> correct answer.

- We work out the answer using <u>logic</u>.

- We don't get a second chance if we make a mistake.

"It is through logic that we prove, but through intuition that we invent."

HENRI POINCARÉ, MATHEMATICIAN

AT A SCHOOL FOR GENIUSES...

We ask QUESTIONS that nobody knows the answer to (yet).

There are LOTS OF POSSIBLE answers.

We find the answer through INTUITION, and by searching and experimenting.

We make lots of ATTEMPTS and MISTAKES, and we're not scared of GETTING IT WRONG.

HOW TO USE THIS BOOK

In this book, ideas bounce around in all directions—just like they do inside our heads! Here's a little guide to help you find your way around.

Quote
Something important said by a genius that still inspires us today.

Everyday tips
Follow these practical tips to develop a "genius attitude" in your everyday life.

MAKE THE ORDINARY
like **RENÉ MAGRITTE** (1898-1967)

If you want to create something brilliant, sometimes it is enough to take very simple things and put them together in a different way. This is how Magritte created his remarkable art.

"To be surreal is to ban the known from the mind and to look for the unnoticed."

The travels of an object
Take an object and photograph it in an unusual place. You'll never see it in the same way again!

YOUR TURN!
✂ **CUT** out about 15 images of objects from magazines.

✂ Have fun putting them together in pairs. Don't stop after the first thought. Keep trying different combinations!

ACTIVITY
Improve your creativity, on your own or with others. These games and activities have lots of different answers, so you can play them over and over and become more of a genius each time!

🏴 Genius snapshot

Discover what made each genius amazing, and how he or she thought differently. It is often only after a genius's death that we realize the contribution they made to their field. So many people mentioned in this book are deceased. You will also find that the majority are male. Keep in mind that women have only had access to higher education from the 20th century onward.

EXTRAORDINARY

René Magritte is one of the masters of Surrealism. For him, the art of painting is the art of thinking, a way of questioning everyday things, and their links to reality. He painted a range of subjects, some of which were very ordinary, in an almost photographic manner, but he assembled them in an unusual way. For example, his painting *Hegel's Holiday* combines two very common objects, an umbrella and a glass of water.

OTHERS WHO MADE THE ORDINARY EXTRAORDINARY

Leonora Carrington (1917-2011) An English-born Mexican surrealist artist and writer, known for her mysterious autobiographical paintings.
Harry Houdini (1874-1926) An American magician famous for his amazing escape acts.
Charles Dickens (1812-1870) An English novelist, considered the best writer of the Victorian Era.
André Breton (1896-1966) A French poet, essayist, critic, and one of the founders of the Surrealist movement.

 THE POWER OF AN IMAGE

What could be more commonplace than a glass and an umbrella? Yet, we are surprised when they are put together in an unusual way. The painting shows the similarities between the objects (water, held in the hand), but also the differences (pulling/pushing, transparent/opaque, concave/convex, rigid/flexible). The title does nothing to enlighten us, instead only deepening the mystery.

 *EXCITING PACKAGING*

The Bulgarian artist Christo wrapped up a variety of things during his career: trees, a bridge, a cathedral, an island, and even the parliament building in Berlin (below). Why? For the sake of art! He claims that his works have no message, but many think his work makes us relook at the beauty of what surrounds us...by hiding it!

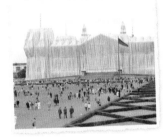

✂ Once you've found some **INTERESTING COMBINATIONS** or "bisociations"—the combination of two things that are unrelated (see p45) - stick each one onto a blank sheet of paper.

The promise

You can give them a mysterious title like Magritte's paintings. *"The titles of the paintings are not explanations and the paintings are not illustrations of the titles."*

BE IMAGINATIVE

THE BRAIN OF A GENIUS

How does a normal human brain work? How is the brain of a genius different? These tips and facts can help you think like a genius and expand your mind.

OTHER GENIUSES

Find out about other people who revolutionized their fields by thinking differently from others.

"It is not doubt, but certainty, which makes a man mad."

FRIEDRICH NIETZSCHE, PHILOSOPHER

"Naivety is the most important attribute of genius."

JOHANN WOLFGANG VON GOETHE, WRITER

"Do one thing every day that scares you."

ELEANOR ROOSEVELT, POLITICIAN

"By knowing how to listen, we possess the brains of others in addition to our own."

LEONARDO DA VINCI, ARTIST AND SCIENTIST

BE CURIOUS

TAKE NOTES

like LEONARDO DA VINCI (1452-1519)

A genius never leaves home without a notebook. It doesn't matter whether it looks cool or not—if it's small, you can carry it around with you everywhere and note down any ideas you have throughout the day!

 NOTE IT!

Creators have lots of ideas, but they never know when they will pop up. This is why its good to carry a notebook. Beatrix Potter, a natural scientist and author of *The Tales of Peter Rabbit*, always carried a notebook with her, in which she would draw and write on topics such as philosophy and politics.

"Look carefully, because what you are going to see is not what you have just seen."

As well as painting the *Mona Lisa*, Da Vinci came up with the idea of the parachute and the helicopter. He was a typical genius and was good at everything: artist, inventor, scientist... But where did all his ideas come from? From his sense of curiosity! Leonardo spent his days observing, wondering, imagining...and jotting everything down in notebooks. Over 7,000 pages written by him have been discovered, but sources claim that he actually had more than twice as many!

Ideas don't spring from nothing

If you "feed" your brain with lots of unusual information, you are more likely to create connections which lead to new ideas!

⟫⟫⟫ page 45 "Make connections"

OTHER GREAT NOTE TAKERS

Grace Hopper (1906-1992) A US Navy rear admiral and pioneer computer scientist who led the team that created the first computer language compiler in the 1950s.

Hypatia (*c.*360-415 CE) A philosopher, astronomer, and mathematician from Alexandria, Egypt.

George Washington Carver (*c.*1860s-1943) An African-American inventor and botanist whose inventions improved the lives of farmers across the world.

Galileo Galilei (1564-1642) An Italian physicist, mathematician, astronomer, and philosopher who played a major role in the Scientific Revolution.

Archimedes (*c.*287-*c.*212 BCE) A Greek mathematician, physicist, engineer, inventor, and astronomer who proved a range of mathematical theories.

Michelangelo (1475-1564) An Italian sculptor, painter, architect, and poet, described as one of the greatest artists of all time.

YOUR NOTEBOOK!

DRAW YOUR LATEST INVENTION!
It doesn't matter if building it would be impossible at the moment. Have faith in the progress of science.

Write down any bits of information that you want to remember (a website, a book, or a place to visit).

Draw whatever is going through your head.

Make a detailed drawing of an idea you have had, to study it more closely.

Note down something that surprised you or made you think.

Note down or stick in unusual information that you find in the news.

www.whatimade.com
A fantastic website run by a man who comes up with wild, yet simple inventions!

An 8-legged cow

My scooter

A vibrating bed
Why does blue bubble bath make white bubbles?

Wi-Fi antenna

airbag

telescopic stand

Why doesn't glue stick to the inside of the bottle?

A python in the pipes
It took firefighters, sanitation workers, and the police more than three hours to dislodge an eight-foot python from the pipes of a building in Miami today.

(source: local newspaper)

OBSERVE

like ALEXANDER FLEMING (1881-1955)

Being a genius is more than just being smart. It means being constantly curious, always observing and seeing what others don't.

THE OBSERVATION GAME

This game will sharpen your observation skills. Play it alone or with others. First, close your eyes and place your finger anywhere on the wheel opposite. Open your eyes, and look around you. Whether you're at home or out and about, **look for something** that...

"Sometimes we find the thing we weren't looking for."

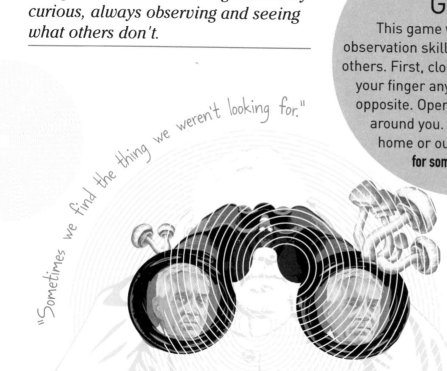

 OTHER GREAT OBSERVERS

Rosalind Franklin (1920-1958) An English chemist who contributed to the discovery of the structure of DNA.

Ada Lovelace (1815-1852) An English mathematician and writer, known as the first computer programmer.

Isaac Newton (1642-1727) An English mathematician, astronomer, author, and physicist, best known for discovering the laws of gravity and motion.

Jane Goodall (b.1934) A British primatologist, anthropologist, and the world's leading expert on chimpanzees.

Max Planck (1858-1947) A German physicist who pioneered quantum physics and won the Nobel Prize in Physics in 1918.

Maria Montessori (1870-1952) An Italian physician and educator, best known for her original education methods, which are used by Montessori teachers around the world.

Many scientific discoveries stem from observation: someone sees something that nobody else has noticed before. Observing some bacterial cultures that he had forgotten about while on vacation, Alexander Fleming noticed a white mold growing on them. Rather than throwing them away, he decided to study their effects. This "penicillium" turned out to be effective against the bacteria that causes several diseases, such as pneumonia and scarlet fever! Fleming had discovered the power of penicillin, now used as an antibiotic, a breakthrough that earned him the Nobel Prize in 1945.

A PHOTOGRAPHIC MIND

Stephen Wiltshire, an artist from the UK, has an astonishing visual memory. After flying over London in a helicopter, he was able to draw the whole city in extreme detail: the drawing took him 5 days! Like many autistic people, Stephen has an extraordinary talent in a specific area, showing the potential of the human mind.

... is black and white
... smells really nice
... comes in pairs
... is yellow
... is shaped like a letter of the alphabet
... has five letters in its name
... is very expensive
... is triangular
... is made in China
... makes a noise
... is red
... is alive
... is old
... is circular
... comes in threes
... has a hidden face
... is heavy
... is soft to touch
... looks like an animal
... starts with the letter C

"Ta da! I've found something that is black and white, soft to the touch, and has a hidden face!"

WHAT WE SEE...

is the brain's primary source of information. So much so that our sight often overrides our other senses!

Try carrying out

a daily activity like eating, washing, or walking with your eyes closed. You'll notice that your other senses seem heightened!

CHALLENGE

Play the observation game with dice. Roll the dice to get a number. Then close your eyes and randomly pick the same number of things from the wheel. Can you find one object that fits all these descriptions?

ASK YOURSELF

like CHARLES DARWIN (1809-1882)

The key characteristic of being a genius is asking yourself questions that no one else has thought of...and searching until you find the answer!

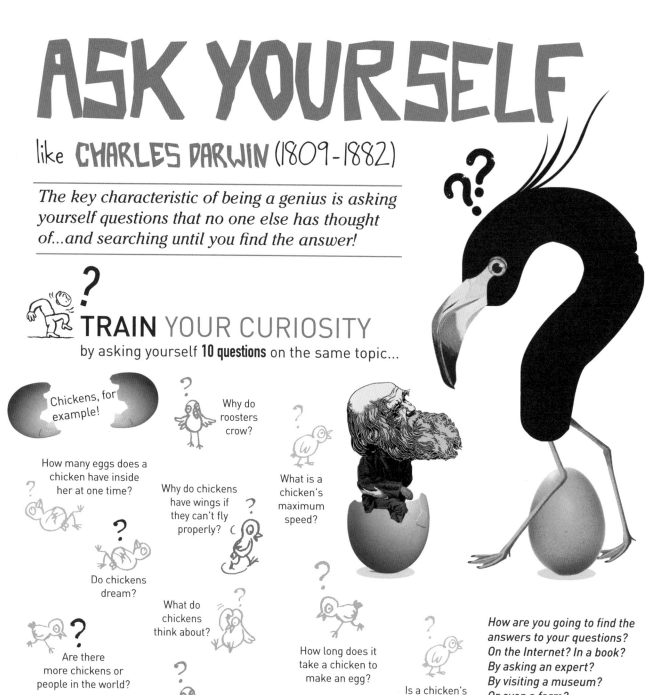

? TRAIN YOUR CURIOSITY

by asking yourself **10 questions** on the same topic...

Chickens, for example!

Why do roosters crow?

How many eggs does a chicken have inside her at one time?

Why do chickens have wings if they can't fly properly?

What is a chicken's maximum speed?

Do chickens dream?

What do chickens think about?

Are there more chickens or people in the world?

How long does it take a chicken to make an egg?

Could the ancestors of chickens fly?

Is a chicken's brain bigger than a pea?

How are you going to find the answers to your questions? On the Internet? In a book? By asking an expert? By visiting a museum? Or even a farm?

Charles Darwin was the first person to suggest that humans were distant relatives of apes (rather than descending from Adam and Eve). During his travels, he wondered why the same species of bird lived on each island he vistited, but they all had very different beaks. He discovered that the beak of each bird was adapted to collecting and eating the food available on its own island. This allowed him to develop his theory of evolution and natural selection: the species that survive are not always the strongest or the smartest, but the ones that are best adapted to their own environment.

QUESTIONS

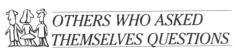

OTHERS WHO ASKED THEMSELVES QUESTIONS

Hildegard of Bingen (1098-1179) A writer, composer, philosopher, and visionary who advised bishops, popes, and kings of the day.

Simone de Beauvoir (1908-1986) A writer, philosopher, political activist, feminist, and social theorist.

Anne Conway (1631-1679) An English philosopher who influenced many of the great thinkers who followed her.

Plato (*c.*428-*c.*348 BC) A philosopher in Classical Greece and teacher of Aristotle.

Rachel Carson (1907-1964) An American marine biologist, author, and conservationist known for her writings on environmental pollution.

Aristotle (384-322 BC) A philosopher and scientist in Ancient Greece.

"A mathematician is a blind man in a dark room looking for a black cat that isn't there."

10 QUESTIONS WITH NO KNOWN ANSWER

There are some questions which have no proven, scientific answer. These can be big questions or little ones. Have fun thinking of them and coming up with your own answers!

A few big questions...

What existed before the Universe?

Why are we alive? What is the purpose of life?

What happens after we die?

... and a few little questions

How did we send a man to the moon before we invented the wheeled suitcase?

Why do we always put bread in the toaster base-down?

Do all animals have dreams?

WHY OR HOW?

We can place all questions on a scale. At the top are the "Why" questions: those that investigate the causes of things, e.g. "Why is the sky blue?". At the very top are the unanswered "Why" questions, e.g. "Why are we here?", which are discussed in philosophy and religion. The "How" questions are at the bottom: these are about solving problems and finding new and better ways of doing things, e.g. "How can we produce renewable electricity?".

The invention of Velcro®

In 1948, a Swiss man named Georges de Mestral wondered why, after a day of hunting, burdock seeds stuck so easily to his clothes. He examined them under the microscope and noticed that the seeds had tiny elastic spikes that clung to the stitches in the fabric. He took this idea and devised two pieces of nylon fabric: one with thousands of tiny loops and the other with thousands of tiny hooks. Velcro® was born!

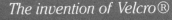

SEE THINGS DIFFERENTLY

like CHARLIE CHAPLIN (1889-1977)

We often say that a film or painting is a work of genius when it offers us a completely new way of looking at something. Here's how you can learn to see things differently.

"It's not the reality in a film that counts, but what your imagination can do with it."

a zoologist
It needs lots
of animals!

WAYS OF LOOKING AT AN IMAGE

Look at a photo, a drawing, or a painting. What's the story behind it? Think of **several answers** and write down your best ideas!

The image below is taken from Chaplin's film *Modern Times*. Even if you're familiar with it, try looking at it with fresh eyes so you can see it differently. Imagine that the image is...

THE ART OF REIMAGINING THINGS

The company BIC wanted to expand its range after making a fortune with the disposable ballpoint pen. Rather than asking "How can we create new and innovative ballpoint pens?" they asked themselves: "How can we create new and innovative disposable objects?". By looking at their company's strengths in a different way, they were able to design disposable razors and lighters, which both sold just as successfully!

OTHERS WHO SAW THINGS DIFFERENTLY

Hedy Lamarr (1914-2000) A Hollywood actress and inventor of the torpedo guidance system.

Quentin Tarantino (b.1963) An American director, writer, and actor who has a star on the Hollywood Walk of Fame for his contributions to the film industry.

Kim Peek (1951-2009) An autistic savant with an amazing memory who inspired the main character in the 1988 film *Rain Man*.

AN INSTRUCTION MANUAL
What is the image trying to explain?

A MUSIC VIDEO
What is the title of the song? What are the lyrics?

A COMIC STRIP
Use speech bubbles to write down what the character is saying or thinking.

A CAMPAIGN POSTER
What cause is it defending? What's the slogan?

AN ADVERTISEMENT
What product or service is being advertised? What is the slogan?

ASK FOR ADVICE
from different people

Imagine that you are going to redesign your bedroom so that it looks completely different. What **advice or ideas** would the people here give you?

an astronaut
What if you hung up some objects to look like zero gravity?

a prehistoric man
Can I paint on the walls?

a police inspector
Secure the space with a code and secret hiding places

a dancer
Add in a big dance floor!

Brain-training game

Each time you use an item in your home (e.g. a shoe, a book, an umbrella, a fork, a sock, a trombone), imagine its other potential uses. This will help you develop your mental flexibility and your ability to innovate!

Why not draw your inventions, to help you visualize how they would look?

As an actor and director, Chaplin created the funny and endearing character known as "The Tramp." At the time, this black and white pantomime figure introduced a new, thought-provoking view of society. For example, his 1936 film *Modern Times* touched upon the bad conditions and pay faced by factory workers. In 1940, in *The Dictator*, he portrayed the dictators Hitler and Mussolini as ridiculous clowns.

FIND ORDER IN DISORDER

like DMITRI MENDELEEV (1834-1907)

"It is the function of science to discover the existence of a general reign of order in nature and to find the causes governing this order."

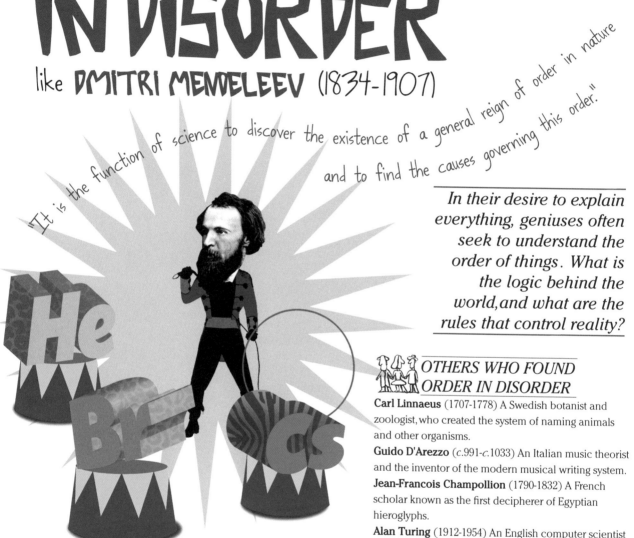

In their desire to explain everything, geniuses often seek to understand the order of things. What is the logic behind the world, and what are the rules that control reality?

OTHERS WHO FOUND ORDER IN DISORDER

Carl Linnaeus (1707-1778) A Swedish botanist and zoologist, who created the system of naming animals and other organisms.

Guido D'Arezzo (*c.*991-*c.*1033) An Italian music theorist and the inventor of the modern musical writing system.

Jean-Francois Champollion (1790-1832) A French scholar known as the first decipherer of Egyptian hieroglyphs.

Alan Turing (1912-1954) An English computer scientist and mathematician who cracked the Enigma code, helping the allies to defeat the Nazis in World War II.

Annie Jump Cannon (1863-1941) An American astronomer who was the first to classify the stars.

Dmitri Mendeleev was a Russian chemist and inventor. He wanted to organize all the chemical elements that make up our universe, including gases and metals. What was his genius idea? The periodic table! The table allowed scientists not only to organize the existing elements based on their atomic mass, but also to predict the existence and properties of other elements that hadn't been discovered yet—like technetium, which was only discovered in 1937, 68 years after the periodic table was created.

WHAT COLLECTION COULD YOU START?

Cube-shaped objects? Red objects? Objects invented in the 20th century? Objects that weigh exactly 100 grams? The options are endless!

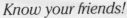

Know your friends!

A great way to get to know a group is to ask people to categorize themselves based on any criteria they want! They will probably start with physical characteristics (e.g. gender, hair color, height, clothing).

Could we classify ourselves based on the number of zits we have?

Ask them to explore features that they can't see: for example, their taste preference (sweet or savory), their families, or their hobbies. This means that each person is likely to experience being in both the majority and the minority depending on the topic. An excellent lesson in tolerance!

LEARN TO THINK BY CATEGORIZING

Humans like to stick labels on everything. Objects, for example, are generally classified based on their use, e.g. leisure, work, cooking, getting dressed. By changing our **classification criteria**, we can throw off the constraints of our normal thinking and learn to think bigger, in terms of "concepts."

Put together a varied collection of about 30 objects (natural and man-made) and categorize them based on at least 10 different criteria.

Size
Material
Name
Smell
Shape
Color
Weight
Price
Function

HEAD FOR THE UNKNOWN

like CHRISTOPHER COLUMBUS (1451-1506)

Geniuses are explorers. They have a passion for discovering what they don't yet know. They need curiosity, but they also need courage to face the unknown!

YOUR RECORD OF DISCOVERIES

Every day, record in a notebook **something new that you have discovered**. You can write it, draw it, stick in a photo or a newspaper article...or even arrange each thing in an alphabetical index like the one below!

A
art
Romanesco broccoli has a repeating pattern that looks like a kaleidoscope.

B
babyfoot
The French word for Table Football

C
citation
"Seriousness is nothing but the filth that accumulates inside empty heads."
(Roland Topor)

D
date
15th October is Global Handwashing Day!
(Unicef)

F
funny
The world championship of melon pip spitting. Record: 69 feet

G
gadget

E
expression
Jargogle!
An old English word that means to confuse or jumble.

H
heart
A human heart beats around 115,000 times each day.

I
image

In 1492, Christopher Columbus set out for India by ship intending to travel west, across the Atlantic. At the time, this was a daring idea—European ships wishing to trade with the Indies always traveled east, around Africa. Columbus did not know how far he would have to travel, or whether there were any other islands along the way. When he landed on San Salvador Island in the Caribbean, he believed that he was in Japan...a belief he held throughout his four voyages!

"Following the light of the sun, we left the Old World..."

※ J ※
joke
At a major economics conference, a professor takes to the stage. "There are three kinds of economists," he says, "those who can count, and those who can't." (Luc de Brabandere)

※ K ※
kitsch

※ L ※
The Louvre
The world's largest art museum, in Paris, France.

※ M ※
music
Erik Mongrain
playing guitar with an unusual technique (seen on YouTube)

※ N ※
name
Mihaly Csikszentmihalyi
(author of a famous psychology book)

※ O ※
origin
The first computer bug was caused by an actual bug (a moth) that got into the machine!

Serendipity
This peculiar word means discovering something good by chance. For this we need curiosity. The geniuses of the past fueled their curiosity by traveling the world. Nowadays, we have the internet!

※ P ※
poetry
I have lived without realizing it. Like grass grows. (Marie Noel)

※ Q ※
question
If vampires don't have reflections, how is their hair always so neat?

※ R ※
recipe
Chorizo and cheese-stuffed peppers.

※ S ※
stories
Suddenly a horse came galloping down the road. It seemed as though the rider had somewhere important to go. A man, who was standing by the road shouted "Where are you going?" The rider replied, "I don't know! Ask the horse!" (Zen story)

※ T ※
technology
Robotic prison guards in South Korea.

※ U ※
uses
If you don't have a comb, use a fork!

※ V ※
vocabulary
It is estimated that a new word enters the English language every two hours!

※ W ※
WC

※ X ※
X

※ Y ※
yourself
Every person has a unique tongue print.

※ Z ※
zeugma
e.g. I have lost my mind and my keys!

OTHERS WHO HEADED FOR THE UNKNOWN

Valentina Tereshkova (b.1937) A Russian cosmonaut, engineer, politician, and the first woman in space.

Gertrude Bell (1868-1926) An English mountaineer, world traveler, and archaeologist, who used her world knowledge to work for the British government during World War I.

Nellie Bly (1864-1922) An American journalist and inventor known for her record-breaking 72-day trip around the world, in 1889-1890.

James Cook (1728-1779) A British explorer, navigator, and captain in the Royal Navy. He was the first European to reach Eastern Australia and Hawaii.

Neil Armstrong (1930-2012) An American astronaut, commander of Apollo 11, and the first person to walk on the Moon, in 1969.

Roald Amundsen (1872-1928) A Norwegian explorer and the leader of the first Antarctic expedition to reach the South Pole, in 1911.

ALEXANDRA DAVID-NEEL
Alexandra David-Neel, an explorer, Buddhist, and anarchist, is known for being the first European woman to visit Lhasa, the sacred capital of Tibet. She traveled there in 1924, disguised as a beggar, as entry was forbidden to foreigners! Alexandra had an overwhelming curiosity about the world. She caught the travel bug at a very early age; at just five years old she went out alone to explore the Bois de Vincennes in Paris. Throughout her life she visited many different countries. Her desire to travel was so strong that she only lived with her husband for a few months!

Alexandra David-Neel

MAKE LINKS

like **BUFFON** (1707-1788)

Geniuses are able to make connections between things that are not obviously linked. They know how to get the most out of their brain, which is like a giant spider's web of linked ideas!

AN ELECTRICAL CIRCUIT CONNECTING 100 BILLION NEURONS

Geniuses don't have more neurons in their brain than the average person, but they do have the ability to make a lot more connections between them! It's this ability that helps them to be inventive.

➡ page 45

Buffon, appointed head of the Jardin des Plantes by Louis XV, and then head of the Cabinet of Natural History, gathered all kinds of plants and animals throughout his life, in order to create an inventory of the entire natural world! *Histoire Naturelle*, his major work, has no less than 36 volumes, even though it only covers minerals and some animals. One of his ideas was to compare animals to humans: he shocked his colleagues by demonstrating how much men looked like apes!

PEN + BALL = ?

One day László Bíró, a Hungarian journalist, was admiring the fast-drying ink used to print newspapers, as it prevented stains caused by smudging. He tried using this ink in a fountain pen, but the thickness of the ink stopped it from flowing. Then he saw some children playing with marbles in a puddle, and noticed that the balls left a trail of water behind them as they rolled. Bíró applied this idea to his problem, putting a ball inside a pen, creating the first biro!

OTHERS WHO MADE LINKS

Louis Pasteur (1822-1895) A French biologist, microbiologist, and chemist known for discovering the processes of vaccination and pasteurization, to prevent disease.

Tim Berners-Lee (b.1955) An English engineer and computer scientist, best known for inventing the World Wide Web in 1989.

Harry Coover (1917-2011) An American chemist who accidentally invented superglue in 1951.

Roy Plunkett (1910-1994) An American chemist who accidentally invented Teflon, a material used in the non-stick coating of pans, in 1938.

Isabella Lucy Bird (1831-1904) An English explorer, writer, and naturalist, and the first woman to be elected Fellow of the Royal Geographical Society.

THE ODD ONE OUT

Choose three pictures from this page at random. Pick the odd one out of the three and say why. You can give several different answers.

They are all mammals, except for the toucan

They all walk on two legs, except for the lion

They all live in the wild, except for the dancer

"We judge, and can only judge, things based on the relationships between them."

TRY IT TOGETHER!

Choose two pictures from this page at random, and compete with a friend to find the most **similarities** between them. You can also play with real objects.

they are both natural

they both start with letters near the beginning of the alphabet

they are both smooth

they often smell good

they both get red in the sun

MAP OUT YOUR IDEAS like your BRAIN!

The human brain is very good at making connections, so what could be more natural than laying out your thoughts as a mental map? It's a great way to explore a subject and come up with ideas!

A MENTAL MAP

Imagine that you want to organize a big party where the theme is "white." Rather than diving right in and randomly thinking of ideas, take the time to **create a mental map**.

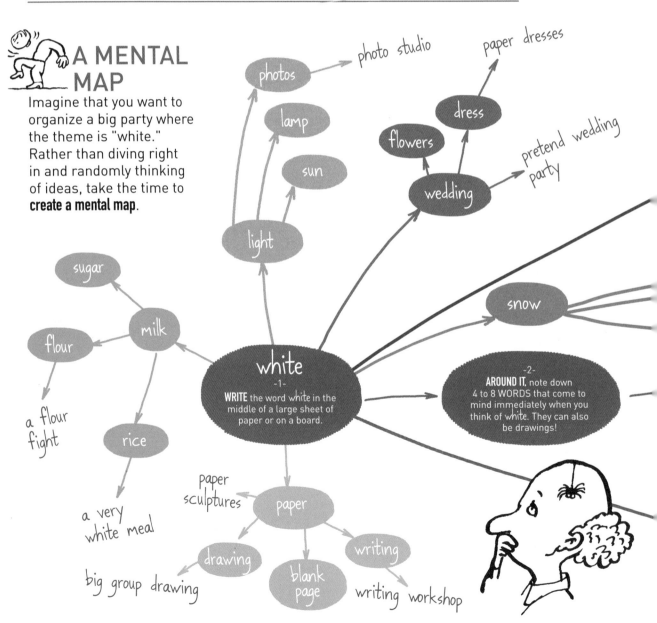

photos → photo studio

paper dresses

dress

flowers

pretend wedding party

wedding

lamp

sun

light

sugar

milk

flour

a flour fight

rice

a very white meal

white
-1-
WRITE the word white in the middle of a large sheet of paper or on a board.

snow

-2-
AROUND IT, note down 4 to 8 WORDS that come to mind immediately when you think of white. They can also be drawings!

paper sculptures

paper

drawing

big group drawing

blank page

writing

writing workshop

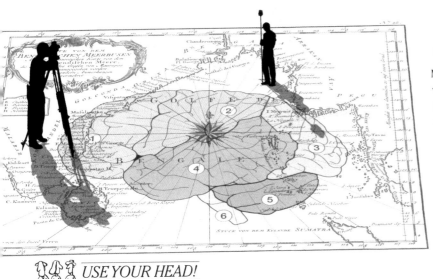

SPIDER'S WEB BRAIN

Making a mental map is the best way to get the most out of your brain. The connections between our 100 billion neurons are like a gigantic 3D spider's web. Yet most of us tend to write our ideas in lists, rather than mental maps, with the ideas coming one after the other, with no connections between them.

USE YOUR HEAD!

This is the title of the 1976 book in which Tony Buzan popularized the concept of the mental map. The main aim? To visually represent the paths that thought takes, making the most of the brain's ability to make connections between ideas.

PRACTICAL USES FOR MENTAL MAPS

- Screenwriters use them to explore film ideas.
- Politicians use them to prepare speeches.
- Students use them to summarize their lessons.

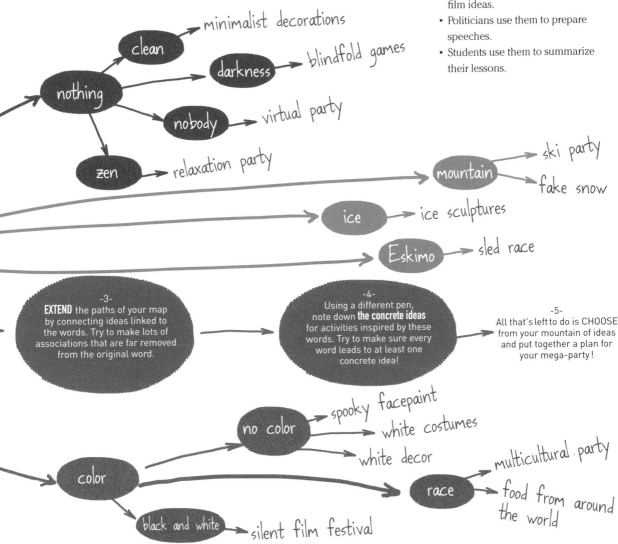

clean → minimalist decorations

darkness → blindfold games

nothing

nobody → virtual party

zen → relaxation party

mountain → ski party, fake snow

ice → ice sculptures

Eskimo → sled race

-3-
EXTEND the paths of your map by connecting ideas linked to the words. Try to make lots of associations that are far removed from the original word.

-4-
Using a different pen, note down **the concrete ideas** for activities inspired by these words. Try to make sure every word leads to at least one concrete idea!

-5-
All that's left to do is CHOOSE from your mountain of ideas and put together a plan for your mega-party!

no color → spooky facepaint, white costumes, white decor

color

race → multicultural party, food from around the world

black and white → silent film festival

DARE TO BE DIFFERENT

"The only difference between myself and a madman is that I am not mad."

like SALVADOR DALI (1904-1989)

Being a genius often starts with a refusal to be "normal." Nothing kills creativity faster than rules and conventional thinking. Certain people dare to be different, sometimes shocking the world in the process...

Just like in his paintings, Salvador Dali went to great lengths to turn his own life into a surrealist work of art. Here are some of his eccentric highlights:

* He once went to the Eiffel Tower restaurant in Paris accompanied by an elephant!
* Invited to give a lecture at the Sorbonne University, he arrived in a Rolls-Royce filled with cauliflowers, which he handed out instead of autographs!
* Asked to design a shop window for a perfume company, Dali arrived on launch day having done no work on the project. He stood in front of the window and threw a rock through it instead!
* He often gave out blank sheets of paper that he had signed, saying: "Here, do a Dali and get rich!"

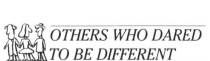

OTHERS WHO DARED TO BE DIFFERENT

Amelia Earhart (1897-disappeared 1937) An American aviation pioneer, author, and the first woman to fly solo across the Atlantic Ocean, in 1932.

David Bowie (1947-2016) An English musician, actor, and leading figure in popular music and culture for over 50 years. Bowie was of one the world's best-selling musicians of all time.

Pythagoras (*c*.570-*c*.495 BCE) A Greek philosopher credited with many pioneering mathematical and scientific discoveries.

Lord Byron (1788-1824) An English nobleman, poet, politician, and flamboyant leading figure in the Romantic movement, regarded as one of the greatest British poets of all time.

Hattie Wyatt Caraway (1878-1950) An American politician who became the first female senator in the United States.

A SURREAL DAY

What if you and your friends decided to have a surreal day like Dali? Who would be the bravest and the most creative?

MIX UP different types of food

chips and jam,
a fruit sandwich,
ice cream and ketchup

backward

hopping

GET AROUND in a strange way

on your hands

USE places differently

play
in a
supermarket

sleep in
a museum

eat in a tree

dance in a
train station

GET CREATIVE in public

make a sculpture
out of leaves
or rubbish

BEING ORIGINAL: WHY BOTHER?

By purposefully acting "abnormally" (doing something that is not "normal" or accepted), some slightly unusual individuals really make us think. When Lady Gaga wore a dress made of raw meat to the 2010 MTV Awards, what point was she trying to make? Did she want to question our meat-eating habits? Was she comparing herself, as a musician, to a piece of meat that record producers "bleed dry" and people "consume"? Or, as she claimed, was she protesting against the way gay people are treated in the US Army? Doing something unusual can make people question bad things in society.

IT'S NOT ALL EASY

Psychologists are fascinated by geniuses. Artists, in particular, often display symptoms of mental illness, sometimes serious conditions such as depression, neurosis, schizophrenia, and psychosis. For them, being creative is often a way of expressing or handling their illnesses.

ORGANIZE a show starring objects

make a chair
do acrobatics

tame
a shoe

tell the tragic
story of a backpack

MAKE A CHANGE

like HERACLITUS (540-480 BCE)

The more we repeat the same habits, the more our attention span and our intelligence starts to stagnate...and the more we fear change! Getting used to change means waking up to something new every day!

OTHERS WHO MADE A CHANGE

Eleanor Roosevelt (1884-1962) An American political figure and activist for human and women's rights, she was the longest serving First Lady and helped to write the Universal Declaration of Human Rights.

Rosa Parks (1913-2005) An activist in the civil rights movement best known for protesting against racial segregation in the Montgomery Bus Boycott in 1955-56.

Sojourner Truth (1797-1883) An African-American activist who escaped slavery and became the first black woman in US history to win a legal battle against a white man for illegal slavery charges.

Emmeline Pankhurst (1858-1928) A political activist and leader of the British suffragette movement, who helped women win the right to vote in 1918.

Susan B. Anthony (1820-1906) An American women's rights activist and pioneer in the women's suffrage movement for equality.

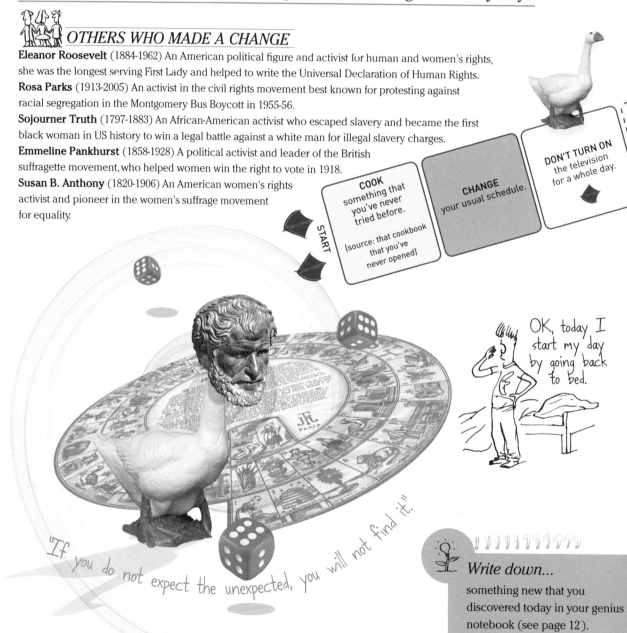

START

COOK something that you've never tried before.

(source: that cookbook that you've never opened)

CHANGE your usual schedule.

DON'T TURN ON the television for a whole day.

OK, today I start my day by going back to bed.

"If you do not expect the unexpected, you will not find it."

Write down...

something new that you discovered today in your genius notebook (see page 12).

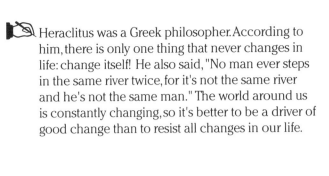

You see! It's very useful for hanging your necklaces on.

And a mirror, is that not useful?

Heraclitus was a Greek philosopher. According to him, there is only one thing that never changes in life: change itself! He also said, "No man ever steps in the same river twice, for it's not the same river and he's not the same man." The world around us is constantly changing, so it's better to be a driver of good change than to resist all changes in our life.

CHANGE how your walls are decorated (make at least two changes).

GET UP 30 minutes earlier than usual.

LIE ON THE GROUND for 5 minutes, alone, in silence, without doing anything.

WEAR clothes that you haven't worn for 6 months.

EAT in a room in which you don't usually eat.

CELEBRATE something— whatever you want!

WATCH a TV show that you think you hate, even though you've never seen it before.

A RISK A DAY SETS YOU ON YOUR WAY!

Give your family this challenge: every day, each of you tries to make at least one of the changes on this page. At the end of the week, each person tells the others what they've learnt from the experience.

TAKE A TRIP to an unknown place. (source: the "What's On" section of your local newspaper).

READ a newspaper or magazine that you've never read.

CHANGE places at the dinner table.

CALL a friend you haven't seen for 6 months.

LISTEN to some new music.

SPEAK to someone you don't know.

TAKE a different route home from school.

Take your family to the library and each **BORROW** one book that you've never read before.

Habits kill creativity

Our brain is a machine built to learn. Once it has discovered a path that allows it to complete a task, it tends to follow the same path repeatedly, as this is the easiest solution.

A CHANGE THAT PAID OFF

Anne-Sophie Pic was only 23 when her father, the chef of a 3-star Michelin restaurant, died. Three years later, the restaurant lost a star. Rather than trying to copy her father, she transformed the resaurant into an ultra-modern destination, reinventing the menu with unusual combinations, such as crème brûlée with foie gras (goose liver) and fish with rhubarb. The result: in 2007, she regained the lost star and became the fourth female chef to achieve a Michelin star rating.

"The only real revolutionary power,
is the power to invent."

JOSEPH BEUYS, SCULPTOR

"Nothing is more dangerous than an idea,
when it's the only one you have."

ALAIN, PHILOSOPHER

"If you can dream it,
you can do it!"

WALT DISNEY, CARTOONIST

"It is harder to crack a
prejudice than an atom."

ALBERT EINSTEIN, PHYSICIST

BE IMAGINATIVE

CONSIDER SEVERAL ANSWERS

like THOMAS EDISON (1847-1931)

At school, many of us learned that there is only one "right" answer. But actually there are often several! Considering alternatives allows us to avoid boring answers and access truly new and original ideas.

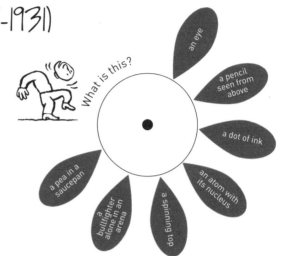

What is this?
- an eye
- a pencil seen from above
- a dot of ink
- an atom with its nucleus
- a spinning top
- a bullfighter alone in an arena
- a pea in a saucepan

"I didn't fail. I just found 10,000 solutions that didn't work."

 ## CAN WE MEASURE CREATIVITY?

Here is a creativity test

conceived by Ellis Paul Torrance in the 1970s. The task is to use circles to draw as many things as possible in 10 minutes. The circle must be the main element of the drawing and it must be possible to identify what you have drawn (nothing abstract). Take the test with your friends and see how creative you are, according to these criteria:

- **FLUIDITY**: did you draw several things?
- **ELABORATION**: did you take an idea and develop it, e.g. draw variations of the same thing?
- **FLEXIBILITY**: are your ideas varied and did you change your point of view, e.g. an egg seen from above, or did you think outside the box, e.g. draw nothing and call it a ball?
- **ORIGINALITY**: did you have any ideas that no one else had?

 Edison is best known as the inventor of the light bulb, but he can also claim to be the inventor of the telephone, cinema, and sound recording. He patented a total of 1,093 inventions during his lifetime! However, his light bulb wasn't created right away. He made several thousand prototypes before succeeding in preventing the filament from burning.

LOOK FOR MULTIPLE ANSWERS

Find at least five right answers to each of these questions.

OTHERS WHO CONSIDERED SEVERAL ANSWERS

Francis Bacon (1561-1626) An English philosopher, statesman, scientist, author, and founder of modern scientific methods.

Stephen Hawking (1942-2018) An English theoretical physicist known for his theories on The Big Bang and black holes.

Alexander Graham Bell (1847-1922) A Scottish scientist and inventor, best known for patenting the first working telephone, in 1876.

Nikola Tesla (1856-1943) A Serbian-American inventor, engineer, physicist, and futurist best known for designing the AC electric system and laying the foundation for wireless technology.

Margaret E. Knight (1838-1914) An American inventor, and holder of 87 patents, she is most noted for inventing the flat-bottomed paper bag in 1871.

What is red and flies?

a butterfly

a robin

a parrot

a firefighting plane

a red ball

a tomato in a helicopter

Ironman

What is green and stings?

What is expensive and smells very bad?

Imagine other riddles by combining two random adjectives!

IMAGINE ✳ THE IMPOSSIBLE

like JOHN LENNON (1940-1980)

To be brilliant is to take the time to dream. Believe that the world can be different, and dare to say your wildest dreams aloud.

What if
men could have babies too
?

What if
people could live
for 300 years
?

John Lennon was one of the four Beatles, undoubtedly the most famous pop group of all time. They composed 275 songs in just 7 years (from 1963 to 1970), each of them so memorable that many artists still sing them to this day. In 1971, Lennon wrote the famous song "Imagine." At the time America was waging a bloody war in Vietnam. Lennon dreamed of a different, peaceful world.

THE WORLD CHANGES THANKS TO THOSE WHO IMAGINE THE IMPOSSIBLE

What if humans walked
on the moon by 1970?
(John F. Kennedy, 1961)

What if black people and white
people had the same rights?
(Martin Luther King, 1963)

What if we could fly an airplane
with solar energy?
(Bertrand Piccard, 2005)

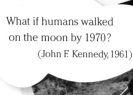

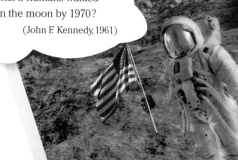

IMAGINE...

Imagine that the world is different. Think about the consequences of each scenario.

What if we didn't need sleep any more ?

What if we all had four arms ?

> How would we be able to cross our arms?
>
> We could shake lots of hands at the same time!

What if we could read other people's thoughts ?

What if everyone on Earth had the same amount of money ?

What if you could choose the characteristics of your baby ?

What if parents had to obey their children ?

What if all metals, struck by a strange virus, became as soft as rubber ?

What if monkeys became smarter than people ?

What if you wrote a 'What if' in your genius notebook every day?

⯈ page 12

What if you could transform everything you touch into chocolate ?

What if you could be in two places at the same time ?

OTHERS WHO IMAGINED THE IMPOSSIBLE

Malala Yousafzai (b.1997) A Pakistani activist who fought for education for females in her home country, and the youngest Nobel Prize winner ever, aged 17.

Harriet Tubman (1822-1913) An American abolitionist and political activist who escaped slavery and risked her life to rescue hundreds of slaves throughout her life.

Mahatma Gandhi (1869-1948) An Indian activist who promoted non-violent protest and led India's independence movement against British rule.

Nelson Mandela (1918-2013) South Africa's first black president who helped end the country's apartheid system of racial segregation.

What if all the colors in the world disappeared ?

BE INSPIRED BY NATURE

like ANTONIO GAUDI (1852-1926)

Geniuses, as we have seen, are curious about everything. Nature is a great source of inspiration for painters, musicians, writers, scientists, and architects like Gaudi.

In Gaudi's work, as in nature, there are no straight lines. Architectural elements—like walls, doors, columns, and even furniture—are very organic and connected like living things. Gaudi developed his style by closely observing nature, and also by studying other buildings, such as Gothic cathedrals and the work of "Art Nouveau" architects, who were in fashion around 1900.

A HOUSE UNLIKE ANY OTHER

Use comparisons with nature to imagine a house that looks unlike any other.

Gather some pictures of nature — animals, plants, minerals...

Think about your chosen image, e.g. a flower. Write down things you associate with it (don't worry about their connection to a house, yet).

- It wilts
- It smells good
- It turns towards the sun
- It has petals
- Bees collect pollen from it
- We make them into bouquets

WHEN TECHNOLOGY COPIES NATURE

Swimming robots with fish tails; spy robots that can fly like bugs; a machine that digs tunnels like a worm; a train with a pointed nose like a bird's beak; a computer network that reacts to a virus attack like a colony of ants...These are just a few examples of "biomimicry"—science that studies nature to improve technology.

THE POWER OF ANALOGY

When Gaudi created a house inspired by nature, he created an analogy: bringing together two different, seemingly unrelated concepts. This shows once again that being creative rarely means inventing something from scratch, but instead creating new connections between things that already exist!
▶page 45

Answers in nature
Think of a problem that concerns you. Go for a walk and stop in front of something in nature that appeals to you. Look at it. How could it relate to your problem? What solutions does it suggest to you?

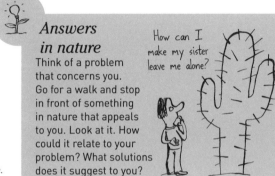

How can I make my sister leave me alone?

OTHERS WHO WERE INSPIRED BY NATURE

Claude Monet (1840-1926) A French artist and founder of the Impressionist movement, famous for his paintings of the countryside.
Emily Dickinson (1830-1886) An American poet whose work was largely unknown during her lifetime.
Georgia O'Keeffe (1887-1986) An American artist and pioneer in the American Modernist movement, best known for her paintings of flowers.
Frida Kahlo (1907-1954) A Mexican artist who painted portraits, self-portraits, and many works inspired by the nature of Mexico.
Antonio Vivaldi (1678-1741) An influential Italian composer and violinist, best known for his composition "Four Seasons," which represents the seasons of the year.

A house that grows at the same rate as a family

People move from one house to another, like bees do with flowers

A house that turns toward the sun

Access the house by flying

Houses grow old and crumble

A bouquet of houses!

Walls made of plants

Look
for ideas for a house unlike any other. Write anything that springs to mind, starting with the words you wrote down.

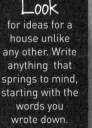

THINK OUTSIDE

like IGOR STRAVINSKY (1882-1971)

A genius is someone who is able to think "outside the box." But what does this mean? To think outside the box we need to think of a problem from a new perspective, and not always take the most obvious answer. This is how geniuses find new ideas and solutions.

HOW DO YOU PUT A PROBE ON MARS WITHOUT DAMAGING IT?

Faced with this problem, NASA engineers first considered traditional solutions such as using parachutes. However, these did not guarantee a smooth landing! They soon came up with a different idea. By wrapping it in a thick layer of inflatable balloons, the probe would bounce when it landed. Once stationary, the balloons could deflate and the probe could set off.

LITTLE EXERCISES TO HELP YOU THINK OUTSIDE THE BOX

The answers lie **far from** where the questions seem to lead...   answers ⟹ page 72

How many ways can you divide a square into 4 equal parts? You might come up with a few answers, but there are an infinite number of way to do this! Look for as many as you can.

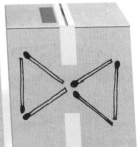

Can you rearrange these six matchsticks to make four identical equilateral triangles?

Hint: Think about perspective!

THE BOX

Russian composer Igor Stravinsky wrote his music by breaking it apart. His best known work is his ballet *The Rite of Spring*, created in 1913. Unlike the classical music of Bach or Mozart, Stravinsky's work sounds unrestrained and resembles a "musical puzzle." When his music was first played in public, some of the audience began to heckle and laugh, but others came forward in his defense. Stravinsky had already left the room. He knew he had just made music history.

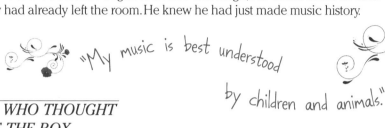

"My music is best understood by children and animals."

OTHERS WHO THOUGHT OUTSIDE THE BOX

Clara Schumann (1819-1896) A German musician and composer, considered one of the best pianists of the time and one of the first to perform from memory.

René Descartes (1596-1650) A French philosopher, mathematician, and scientific thinker who has been called the father of modern philosophy.

Caroline Herschel (1750-1848) A German astronomer who discovered over 2,400 astronomical objects and was the first woman to be awarded a Gold Medal of the Royal Astronomical Society.

Wolfgang Mozart (1756-1791) An influential Austrian composer who started writing classical music at the age of five.

Elon Musk (b.1971) A South African-born American business magnate, engineer, and the brains behind many pioneering companies, including SpaceX and Tesla.

 Riddles

Can you name 3 consecutive days without saying Monday, Tuesday, Wednesday, Thursday, Friday, Saturday, or Sunday?

A police officer sees a truck driver going the wrong way down a one-way street. But she does not arrest him. Why?

There are six eggs in a basket. Six people each take an egg. Why is there still one egg left in the basket?

Three glasses are filled with juice, and three are empty. By moving only one glass, can you arrange them so that empty and full glasses alternate?

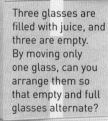

A farmer goes to a garden centre to buy 10 apple trees.

The owner tells him, "If you can plant the 10 apple trees in 5 rows of 4, I'll give them to you for free."

How can the farmer do it?

Connect these nine dots using four straight lines. Your pencil must not leave the paper and each point can only be crossed once.

If you know the answer to this well-known challenge, can you connect all the dots with only three lines or even just a single line?

A London hairdresser says he would rather cut the hair of three people from Manchester than one from London. Why?

TURN THINGS ON THEIR HEAD

like NICOLAUS COPERNICUS (1473-1543)

Many discoveries have been made because someone dared to think "against" what was normal in their time. This is a good method for finding really original ideas.

"...in the middle of everything is the Sun."

OXYMORONS

Creativity is sometimes sparked from thinking about opposites. This idea is known as an "oxymoron." Below are some examples, have fun coming up with your own—make them as funny as you can!

"A dark light"
"Baggy tights"
"A gigantic dwarf"
"Seriously crazy"

In the Middle Ages, most people believed that the Earth was the center of the Universe, and that the Sun, Moon, and stars all moved around it. The Polish astronomer Nicolaus Copernicus used calculations to prove that it is actually the Earth that orbits the Sun! This theory changed people's ideas about the world (the "Copernican revolution") and even the Church finally accepted it, in 1750!

OTHERS WHO TURNED THINGS ON THEIR HEAD

Benjamin Franklin (1706-1790) A leading author, politician, scientist, inventor, and one of the Founding Fathers of the United States, who invented the lightning rod and bifocal glasses and made many discoveries relating to electricity.

William Shakespeare (1564-1616) An English poet, playwright, and actor, viewed as the greatest writer in the English language.

Emmy Noether (1882-1935) One of the leading and most creative mathematicians of her time, she developed theories in both math and physics, including Noether's theorem.

Immanuel Kant (1724-1804) An influential German philosopher.

IMAGINE AN EXTRAORDINARY TABLE

List the main characteristics of a table.

What would a table that has **NONE** of these characteristics look like?
- no legs
- a non-horizontal surface
- a non-geometric form

Draw your ideas
and then look at some examples ➠ page 73

Normally, a table has...

legs

a geometric form

a horizontal surface

Apply this "table" exercise to other subjects such as:

a meal, a school, a declaration of love, parents, politeness...

List all the "usual" characteristics of these subjects; then imagine solutions that do not contain any of these characteristics.

SWITCH IT UP

At the 1968 Olympics in Mexico City, US athlete Dick Fosbury won gold at the high jump by jumping backward over the bar! Up until then, all athletes crossed the bar with a forward roll style. Today, the "Fosbury flop" is the only technique used in competition.

TRY COMBINATIONS

like JOHANNES GUTENBERG (1400-1468)

Geniuses are jugglers. They have a lot of knowledge and know how to combine it in wondrous new ways that seem completely random to normal people.

$$1 + 1 = 3$$

Many inventions are the result of combining **two existing ideas** in a way they never have been before!

OTHERS WHO TRIED COMBINATIONS

James Watt (1736-1819) A Scottish inventor who improved the design of the steam engine, which contributed to the Industrial Revolution.

Philo Farnsworth (1906-1971) An American inventor who developed the first electronic TV, by taking cathode ray tubes and combining them with a way to scan images using electrons.

Katharine Burr Blodgett (1898-1979) An American scientist who invented non-reflective glass used for camera lenses, eyeglasses, car windshields, and computer screens.

Christopher Latham Sholes (1819-1890) An American inventor who took the idea of a printing press and developed the first personal typewriter.

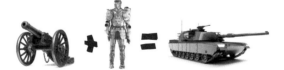

CHALLENGE

You are spending the weekend in a cabin in the woods. All you have at your disposal are the objects below:

How do you catch a wild boar? make a fire? cut meat? make music? protect yourself from thieves? or draw water from a well?

Your turn!

Imagine what you could invent by randomly combining two images.
It could be an object, a service, a work of art...

cat jewelry

a ring shaped like a cat that purrs when stroked

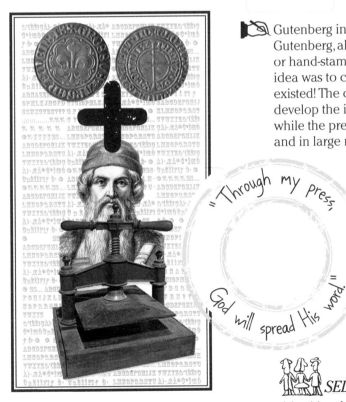

"Through my press, God will spread His word."

Gutenberg introduced printing to Europe. Before Gutenberg, all books had to be written out by hand or hand-stamped with wooden blocks. His brilliant idea was to combine two techniques that already existed! The coin printing system inspired him to develop the idea of removable metal characters, while the press made it possible to print efficiently and in large numbers.

BISOCIATION

Many geniuses possess the ability to connect two things that belong to very different worlds. The term "bisociation" was created by Arthur Koestler in his book *The Cry of Archimedes*.

SELLING PRODUCTS

Advertising often makes a visual link between a product and something which enhances it. Here, soft butter becomes a powerful wave.

BE INSPIRED BY THE PAST

like PABLO PICASSO (1881-1973)

To have brilliant ideas we should not expect to create something out of nothing. True geniuses are able to draw inspiration from the works of masters who preceded them.

REWORK A CLASSIC

Here are some ideas to help you **become creative**, using the work of **great creators**!

RECOMPOSE

Cut a full-color copy of the painting into pieces. Arrange these pieces to make another picture.

First choose a classic painting (such as *Landscape with the Fall of Icarus* by Bruegel—above). Make several photocopies of it in black and white.

MIX
two paintings

Trace the main lines of your painting onto another sheet and then color in using the colors from another famous painting (e.g. a work by Joan Miró).

SIMPLIFY

Trace the painting with lines and simple forms. Then color it in using only the three primary colors (yellow, red, and blue) plus black and white.

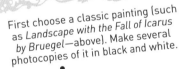

MUSIC COVERS

Musicians love to revisit classics too. According to the Guinness Book of Records, "Yesterday" by the Beatles (1964) is the most widely covered song of all time.

CHANGE THE DIMENSIONS

Try coloring in a photocopy with oil pastels, and then tear it up into several pieces! Create something on paper with the torn pieces. Make some parts in 3D, raised off the page.

In 1907, Picasso visited an exhibition of African masks and statues in Paris. Struck by this way of representing the human figure, using simple angles and shapes, he locked himself in his studio for three months and produced *Les Demoiselles d' Avignon*, the scandalous painting that marked the beginning of Cubism.

Picasso hated repeating himself so he changed his style a few years later, exploring a much more classical genre, before again continuing his exploration of simpler lines and expressive forms. Toward the end of his life, after having tried many painting styles, Picasso turned to the old masters. Fascinated by Velasquez's *Las Meninas*, he painted over 50 versions, each with a distinctive Picassian stamp.

"Success is dangerous. We start to copy ourselves, and copying yourself is more dangerous than copying others...it's sterile."

OTHERS WHO WERE INSPIRED BY THE PAST

Wilbur (1867-1912) & **Orville Wright** (1871-1948) American aviation pioneers who were the first to achieve controlled flight in a heavier-than-air aircraft, in 1903.

Bob Dylan (b.1941) An American singer and songwriter, influenced by Country and Western, Rock 'n' Roll, and Folk music, and winner of the Nobel Prize for Literature in 2016.

George Orwell (1903-1950) An English writer, famous for his novels *Animal Farm* and *Nineteen Eighty-four*, whose work spoke out about social injustice in society.

Audrey Flack (b.1931) An American painter and sculptor who pioneered the art genre of photorealism.

MAKE THE ORDINARY

like **RENÉ MAGRITTE** (1898-1967)

If you want to create something brilliant, sometimes it is enough to take very simple things and put them together in a different way. This is how Magritte created his remarkable art.

"To be surreal is to ban the known from the mind and to look for the unnoticed."

The travels of an object
Take an object and photograph it in an unusual place. You'll never see it in the same way again!

YOUR TURN!

 CUT out about 15 images of objects from magazines.

- - - > Have fun putting them together in pairs. Don't stop after the first thought. Keep trying different combinations!

EXTRAORDINARY

René Magritte is one of the masters of Surrealism. For him, the art of painting is the art of thinking, a way of questioning everyday things, and their links to reality. He painted a range of subjects, some of which were very ordinary, in an almost photographic manner, but he assembled them in an unusual way. For example, his painting *Hegel's Holiday* combines two very common objects, an umbrella and a glass of water.

OTHERS WHO MADE THE ORDINARY EXTRAORDINARY

Leonora Carrington (1917-2011) An English-born Mexican surrealist artist and writer, known for her mysterious autobiographical paintings.

Harry Houdini (1874-1926) An American magician famous for his amazing escape acts.

Charles Dickens (1812-1870) An English novelist, considered the best writer of the Victorian Era.

André Breton (1896-1966) A French poet, essayist, critic, and one of the founders of the Surrealist movement.

THE POWER OF AN IMAGE

What could be more commonplace than a glass and an umbrella? Yet, we are surprised when they are put together in an unusual way. The painting shows the similarities between the objects (water, held in the hand), but also the differences (pulling/pushing, transparent/opaque, concave/convex, rigid/flexible). The title does nothing to enlighten us, instead only deepening the mystery.

EXCITING PACKAGING

The Bulgarian artist Christo wrapped up a variety of things during his career: trees, a bridge, a cathedral, an island, and even the parliament building in Berlin (below). Why? For the sake of art! He claims that his works have no message, but many think his work makes us relook at the beauty of what surrounds us...by hiding it!

 Once you've found some **INTERESTING COMBINATIONS** or "bisociations"—the combination of two things that are unrelated (see p45) - stick each one onto a blank sheet of paper.

The promise

You can give them a mysterious title like Magritte's paintings. *"The titles of the paintings are not explanations and the paintings are not illustrations of the titles."*

VISUALIZE

like ALBERT EINSTEIN (1879-1955)

It is often assumed that the greatest scientists and mathematicians think only in terms of words and numbers. Nothing could be further from the truth! The greatest minds visualize their theories as mental pictures.

The physicist Albert Einstein worked on complex hypothetical ideas. Because of this he needed to use images and metaphors in order to develop his theories on time and space, which were only confirmed with practical experiments many years later. He imagined, for example, riding a ray of light in space; or he asked himself questions such as: "If I'm in a free-falling elevator and I drop a coin, will it fall to the ground, stay in midair, or travel up to the ceiling?"

THE MAN WHO CAN "SEE" NUMBERS

Daniel Tammet can recite the number Pi (3.1416...) to the 22,514th decimal! In his book *Embracing the Wide Sky*, he states that he "sees numbers as complex shapes, in 3D, with color and texture."

YOU'LL SEE!

Here are some visualization exercises, from the amateur to the professional!

1. Realistic visualizations

- **Start by visualizing elements of reality**: Visualize an apple in detail.
- **Travel into the past**: Visualize your first ever bedroom. Take time to observe all the details: furniture, decoration, materials, and textures.
- **Travel in space**: Visualize a large object (e.g. your house) and turn it around. Look at it from above, from different sides, go inside...

Go somewhere quiet, close the door, and turn off your mobile phone. Sit somewhere comfortable and relax. Breathe in and out deeply.

So, did you manage it? WELL DONE! You have just done what no machine can do: travel in time and space without moving!

THE SENSE OF SIGHT

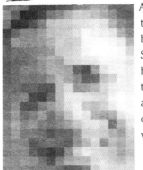

Ask a computer to recognize this image and it won't be able to—but you can! Studies of the human brain have shown that our ability to record and store images is almost unlimited. A third of our cerebral cortex handles visual information!

OTHER GREAT VISUALIZERS

Katherine Johnson (b. 1918) An African-American mathematician who, despite racial prejudice, calculated the flight paths of NASA spacecraft for over 30 years, helping to send astronauts to the Moon.
Jeff Hanson (b. 1993) An award-winning visually-impaired artist who uses bold colors and textures to create his striking paintings.
Niels Bohr (1885-1962) A Danish physicist who received the Nobel Prize for his role in the development of quantum physics.
Frank Lloyd Wright (1867-1959) An American architect who designed over 1,000 structures in his lifetime.

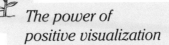

The power of positive visualization

To increase their chances of success, many sportspeople, public speakers, and dancers prepare by imagining they are performing every part of their upcoming task perfectly. But the reverse is also true: if you really think you're going to fail, you increase the chances of that happening.

"Imagination is more important than knowledge. For knowledge is limited, while the imagination embraces the entire universe."

2. Imaginary visualizations

• Visualize an apple and mentally transform it: change the shape, the size, make it disappear and reappear.
• **Travel into the future**: imagine climbing a hill, and from the top you can see yourself in five years. Where are you? What are you doing?
• **Travel in your desires**: visualize something you really want. For example, if you dream of writing a book imagine its shape, its cover, its title, and what is written on the back. This will increase your chances of finding inspiration to write it! Why? Because it is easier to aim for something specific than something vague. In the same way, imagine a trip, a pet, and why not the love of your life?!

3. For visualization pros

• **Imaginary journey**
Lie down on a rug with a friend. Close your eyes. Imagine it's a flying carpet and go on a trip. The first person begins to describe what they see. The other person should follow, by adding details. You are experiencing an extraordinary journey...

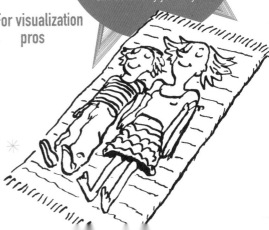

TRUST YOUR SUBCONSCIOUS

like SIGMUND FREUD (1856-1939)

Sometimes the best way to look for great ideas...is to not look for them at all! Instead let them come to you from the depths of your subconscious.

"A dream is the satisfaction of a desire."

Up until the 19th century, dreams were considered either predictions of the future or messages from the gods (or demons) that had to be interpreted. Then Freud arrived. The inventor of psychoanalysis explained that dreams are simply the voice of our subconscious. During sleep, our mind expresses all the desires and fears that our consciousness has repressed during the day. The dream world is so inspiring that many great minds consciously seek access to it so they can use dreams for ideas.

"In psychoanalysis, we practice the same idea as automatic writing, but with speech...it aims at better understanding and relieving our inner suffering."

Leon Spilliaert, *Vertigo*, 1908

HERE ARE SOME **ACTIVITIES** TO HELP YOU ACCESS **YOUR** SUBCONSCIOUS

They all have a common goal: to **ignore reason** and self-control, and to let ideas express themselves freely.

AUTOMATIC WRITING

Work like a surrealist writer, by placing yourself in front of a page and writing without stopping for 15 to 30 minutes. Work quickly, without thinking or worrying about meaning or grammar. This exercise is a wonderful way to relax, to be imaginative, and to get to know yourself!

LOSE CONTROL

Take some paper and a pencil and close your eyes. Let your pencil run over the paper freely. Open your eyes and, from this chaos, try to see an image of a character, an animal, or anything you want. Or why not try drawing with your weaker hand? While the right hand is connected to the left hemisphere of the brain (logical and analytical), the left is connected to the right half of the brain, which deals with imagination and creativity!

HOW TO REMEMBER DREAMS?

DO NOT GET UP immediately: being in the state of half-sleep gives us the best chance of remembering our dreams!
NOTE DOWN your dreams, so that your brain gets used to remembering them!

LOOK FOR IDEAS IN DREAMS

Robert Louis Stevenson found the plot of *Doctor Jekyll and Mr. Hyde* in a dream. Richard Wagner dreamed the music for his opera *Tristan and Isolde*, and Friedrich August Kekule discovered the structure of the benzene molecule, in the form of a ring of 6 snakes biting their own tails! There was nothing magical about it: all these people were thinking hard about a problem, and during sleep, the elements of the problem were free to organize themselves and provide a solution.

USE CHANCE

Ask someone to give you a random object. Quickly find at least three things in common between you and this object.

Try with other objects, or images. Chance is a powerful way to access the unexpected.

I'm like a spoon...

In a spoon's reflection I can see myself the right way up, or upside down. I also like to change my point of view!

I like to let others experience or "taste" what has inspired me!

OTHERS WHO TRUSTED THEIR SUBCONSCIOUS

Mary Whiton Calkins (1863-1930) An American philosopher and psychologist, and the first woman to become president of the American Psychological and Philosophical Associations.
Margaret Floy Washburn (1871-1939) A leading American psychologist and the first woman to be granted a PhD in psychology.
Carl Jung (1875-1961) An influential Swiss psychologist and psychiatrist who developed many theories on personality types and unconscious thought.
Nostradamus (1503-1566) A French astrologer and physician who made many predictions and prophecies about the future.

OPENING THE DOOR TO OUR SUBCONSCIOUS

Ideas emerge from chaos, and can take surprising and even incomprehensible forms. One thing is certain: if an image is scary or worrying, don't keep it to yourself—talk about it with someone!

"When I work, I relax. Doing nothing or entertaining visitors makes me tired."

PABLO PICASSO, ARTIST

"Discipline is the key."

TOMI UNGERER, AUTHOR AND ILLUSTRATOR

"Success consists of going from failure to failure without losing enthusiasm."

WINSTON CHURCHILL, POLITICIAN

"Just as appetite comes by eating, so work brings inspiration."

IGOR STRAVINSKY, MUSICIAN

"If you're not failing every now and again, it's a sign you're not doing anything very innovative."

WOODY ALLEN, FILMMAKER

BE DETERMINED

CREATE CONSTANTLY
like MARCEL PROUST (1871-1922)

As the old saying goes, "Rome wasn't built in a day". There are only three foolproof ways to turn a good idea into a work of genius: work, work, and...work.

"Art allows us to glimpse multiple worlds beyond our own. However many original artists there are, we have just as many potential worlds open to us."

7 DESCRIPTIONS of a treat: e.g. a chocolate egg.

THANK YOU

7 THANK YOUS to things in your life.

THANK YOU to my eyes, my optic nerves, and my brain for allowing me to read.

Like many writers, Marcel Proust was a hard worker. There is nothing mysterious about it: writing a masterpiece like his series of novels *In Search of Lost Time*—which features more than 200 characters over four generations—requires time, solitude, and hard work. From 1907 to 1919, Proust was shut in his room in Paris, working at night, sleeping during the day, and occasionally dining out with friends. He neglected his health, to the extent that he passed away at the age of 51 from an untreated bout of bronchitis.

THANK YOU to the inventor of marshmallows, which are so yummy!

THANK YOU to my chair which supports me and my bottom.

OTHERS WHO CREATED CONSTANTLY

William Shakespeare (1564-1616) An English poet, playwright, and actor who wrote 37 plays and 154 sonnets during his career.

Paul McCartney (b. 1942) A British musician and member of The Beatles, who has written the most No.1 songs of all time.

Enid Blyton (1897-1968) An English children's writer whose books are among the world's best-sellers. She wrote 762 books in her lifetime.

Stephen King (b. 1947) An American author of horror and supernatural fiction, who has published 54 novels which have sold millions of copies across the world.

Virginia Woolf (1882-1941) An English writer, thought to be one of the most important modern authors, and a pioneer in the use of non-linear narrative.

EUREKA, I FOUND IT!

Sometimes, although we work really hard, our ideas just don't flow. Henri Poincaré, a great scientist and mathematician, analyzed his process of invention. He identified four steps:

· PREPARATION: he worked intensely on a subject that interested him, but failed to find a solution despite his research.

· INCUBATION: he then went out for a walk and stopped thinking about his problem.

· ILLUMINATION: while he was walking, the solution struck him like a flash of lightning!

· VERIFICATION: he then went home, checked his solution, and finished his work.

This shows that our brain continues to work on a problem, even if we are not aware of it.

GYMNASTICS FOR WRITERS

To become a writer, you have to write! In the following 7 challenges, you'll be faced with a writing task with a constraint. Give yourself just 7 minutes to complete each task. Try them and you'll see how **constraints can stimulate creativity** and give you a taste for writing!

7 SENTENCES each with just 7 words to describe the beginning of your day.

7 POWERS that you dream of having.

7 WORDS chosen at random from 7 books. Write a paragraph that contains them all.

It's been exactly 273 days since my head was separated from my body.

7 OPENING LINES of novels that do not exist (and that you will probably never write).

Mrs. Ceramic had never liked chocolate desserts.

Donald's feet were hovering four inches from the ground, and only his dog seemed surprised.

7 DECLARATIONS OF LOVE for your pen (the one you're holding in your hand)!

HAVE BIG PLANS

like MARTIN LUTHER KING (1929-1968)

Geniuses have a vision. They see beyond what is "normal" and know that the world can be different. Their dream becomes an inspiration for millions of people.

 Segregation of white people and black people, in schools, restaurants, and trains, and a ban on interracial couples was the reality in the southern United States in the 1950s. Following the arrest of a woman of color who refused to give up her seat for a white man on the bus, a young pastor gradually became the figurehead of a peaceful movement of "civil disobedience." His name was Martin Luther King. He wanted to go much further: his aim was to gain true equal rights for people of color.

Martin Luther King had many enemies, and was assassinated in 1968. But forty years later, in 2008, Barack Obama became the first African-American president of the United States. This was the message of Martin Luther King's famous "I have a dream" speech, given in 1963:

"I have a dream...that my four little children will one day live in a nation where they will not be judged by the color of their skin, but by the content of their character."

OTHERS WHO HAD BIG PLANS

Abraham Lincoln (1809-1865) President of the USA who successfully campaigned to end slavery in the United States, in 1865.

Karl Marx (1818-1883) A German revolutionary sociologist who believed that capitalism would eventually collapse into an equal, classless society.

Gloria Steinem (b. 1934) An American feminist, political activist, writer, and spokeswoman for the American feminist movement in the '60s and '70s.

Nelson Mandela (1918-2013) South Africa's first black president who helped end the country's apartheid system of racial segregation.

WHAT WERE HIS DREAMS?

Why did millions of people mourn the death of Steve Jobs, head of Apple, in 2011? Because this brilliant businessman was also a visionary who gave them things they had never dared to dream of. The man who created the iMac, the iPod, the iPhone, and the iPad didn't ask himself "How can I improve what already exists?". Instead, he asked "How can I create products that make consumers' dreams come true?".

The LADDER OF IDEAS

How could you plan to increase your own happiness? And what do you want to do to improve the world? Make a list using the ladder of ideas.

THE BROKEN LADDER

For average people, imagining the impossible is pointless, because it's impossible! But researchers have identified the main obstacles to creativity: fear of the unknown, risk, and failure. So don't let your mind be constrained by what is possible.

SKY IDEAS
We're in dreamland! These ideas are technically or physically impossible, but they can be inspiring!

What would increase your happiness?

being a bird

living in the 1960s

having hands that can heal any illness

What would improve the world?

inventing 100%-renewable energy

MOUNTAIN IDEAS
These are achievable, but more difficult: you will need effort, time, equipment, or money.

cycling across Europe

What would increase your happiness?

learning to draw manga comics

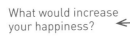

Me? I don't have dreams.

But at least I won't be disappointed.

What would improve the world?

making a film to educate parents

planting a forest

What would increase your happiness?

calling a friend

snoozing in the sun

EARTH IDEAS
These are very easy ideas that can be achieved right away.

smiling at 3 people each day

What would improve the world?

taking a bike rather than a car

WORK METHODICALLY
like AGATHA CHRISTIE (1890-1976)

Every genius has his or her own "recipe" for working efficiently. Let yourself be inspired by other people's tips and tricks and then find your own way of working!

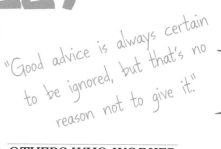

"Good advice is always certain to be ignored, but that's no reason not to give it."

THE ENEMY: PROCRASTINATION

Have you heard of it? This is the tendency to put things off and postpone them until tomorrow. A golden tip: If you have a big project (so big that it scares you), work on it right now, for an hour or two. Then stop and come back to it later. The little seed that you have planted in your mind will grow, even without you realizing it. Also, the task won't seem as big once you've made that first step.

OTHERS WHO WORKED METHODICALLY

Florence Nightingale (1820-1910) A British nurse in charge of caring for soldiers during the Crimean War. She founded modern nursing and established the first scientifically based nursing school.

Magnus Carlsen (b. 1990) A Norwegian chess grandmaster who earned his grandmaster title at just 13 years old.

Edgar Allen Poe (1809-1849) An American writer and literary critic, best known for his dark and mysterious poems and short stories, and said to be the inventor of the detective fiction genre.

Marie Curie (1867-1934) A Polish-born French physicist and chemist, famous for her work on radioactivity, and the first woman to win a Nobel Prize, in 1903 for physics.

Some creative secrets

These examples will help you to find your own way of working on your brilliant project.

Choose the right time

After spending the day running his impressive empire, **Napoleon Bonaparte** would work at night on files that required a lot of concentration, such as the drafting of his famous Civil Code. Many writers say they are very inspired early in the morning, before breakfast, or late at night.

Eeeeww! That's disgusting.

Choose the place

The painter **Pierre Soulages** lives in the hills above the French Riviera, with magnificent views. However he chooses to paint in a windowless studio, so he is not distracted by the beautiful landscape. For more than 20 years, he painted only with black paint!

Agatha Christie had her own specific method for writing detective novels. The story would come to her in unexpected places, like on the street or in a tram. She would build her story starting with the crime: the murder weapon, the murderer, and the motive. Then she'd bring in the other suspects and their motives. Finally she would add clues and false leads to confuse the reader. When everything was in place in her mind, she would start writing. Often she was writing two books at the same time, so if she ran out of ideas for one book she could work on the second one.

Find your own method

The writer **Vladimir Nabokov** wrote standing up, with his text stuck up to the wall. This way, he could move the paper around at any time and change the structure of the story.

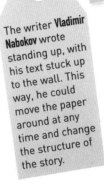

Observe regular hours

Every morning, at 9 am sharp, **René Goscinny** (the writer of Asterix) would write the texts for his comic books. At noon he would eat and then leave for the editorial office of *Pilote* magazine, where he was editor-in-chief.

Dare to say no

To concentrate fully, you need to make sure you're not disturbed. The great philosopher and mathematician **René Descartes** traveled alone from city to city, never indicating in his letters exactly where he was.

I'm undercover.

Grrr...and ten!

Give yourself a tangible goal

Like many authors, **Stephen King** writes at least 10 pages every day, even if he's on vacation!

PERSEVERE

like VINCENT VAN GOGH (1853-1890)

Of course, it takes more than a couple of successes to become a recognized genius. But how many failures does it take before you reach success? Some people think the secret of success is daring to make mistakes.

 Everyone knows about Vincent Van Gogh, his paintings are among the most expensive in the world! But how did his career start? He began as an employee of an art dealer at age 16, but he was soon fired (he was upset that art was being treated as a commodity). He then tried to become a pastor, but again he failed, despite his great faith. Van Gogh then decided he wanted to learn how to draw, but he found the techniques difficult. He spent five years tearing up hundreds of drawings, before achieving a personal style with *The Potato Eaters* in 1885. He then went to France where he painted passionately for the last five years of his life. He would sell only one painting during his whole lifetime.

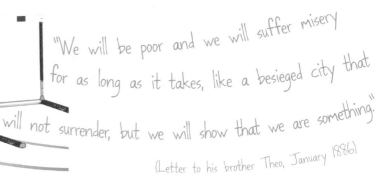

"We will be poor and we will suffer misery for as long as it takes, like a besieged city that will not surrender, but we will show that we are something."

(Letter to his brother Theo, January 1886)

A GALLERY OF FAILURES...*who finally succeeded!*

The parents of ALBERT EINSTEIN were told that their son was mentally backward. He is today recognized as one of the greatest geniuses that ever lived on Earth.

THE BEATLES were refused a contract by Decca records, who didn't like their sound, and thought that guitar bands were going out of fashion. EMI believed in them and they became the greatest band of all time.

The basketball star MICHAEL JORDAN was thrown off his school basketball team because of "lack of talent."

EUREKA, I ~~FAILED~~ TRIED AGAIN!

Make a list of everything you've tried and failed to achieve.
If your list includes over ten items, you should win a **risk taking medal**!

Nothing sold!

My exhibition

of carved potatoes
(priced $250 to $1,500).

My recipe

—fish with cheese
and strawberry jam.

Nobody touched
it and we threw
it all away!

- They can be inspirational
- At least10 failures before a success is normal!
- You could make an unexpected discovery
- Have the courage to make more mistakes
- You can learn something

MISTAKES
FAILURES
ATTEMPTS
EXPERIENCES
TRIES
INITIATIVES

My epic novel

in 10 volumes. So far
I have written just
one sentence.

I'm waiting
for inspiration
for the second.

There are lots
of things I've
succeeded in...

...not completely
failing at!

OTHERS WHO PERSEVERED

Helen Keller (1880-1968) An American author, political activist, and lecturer who was the first deaf-blind person to earn a university degree.

Elizabeth Blackwell (1821-1910) The first woman to receive a medical degree in America and the first woman to be on the UK medical register.

Mary Jackson (1921-2005) An aeronautical engineer and mathematician who was the first African-American female engineer to work at NASA.

Oprah Winfrey (b.1954) An American television personality, actress, entrepreneur, and one of the richest and most influential women in the US, who was fired for being "unfit for television" early in her career.

Bill Gates (b.1955) An American computer programmer and entrepreneur who co-founded Microsoft Corporation, but whose very first business failed.

"Do something every day that scares you."
Thanks to this wise advice from Eleanor Roosevelt, you will develop your "risk muscles," and you'll dare to make mistakes!

page 27

In 1947, a producer from 20th Century Fox released MARILYN MONROE from her contract after just a year, because he found her "unattractive" and thought she didn't know how to act. The American actress became one of the most famous Hollywood stars of all time.

Unfortunately, the reverse can also be true. Some very famous and brilliant people end up in poverty. GEORGES MÉLIÈS, a special effects pioneer of the silent movie era, directed almost 600 films. But in 1913 his luck changed, with the death of his wife, financial problems, and the beginning of World War I. He ended up burning a large number of his films and finished his career as a toy seller in Paris.

WORK AS A TEAM

like WALT DISNEY (1901-1966)

A real genius knows that several heads are better than one. So never hesitate to organize brainstorming sessions to come up with ideas.

How did Walt Disney create his cartoon masterpieces, such as *Snow White, Fantasia,* and *Pinocchio*? He worked with a team! One of his great talents was being able to "gather talent" around him. Everyone within his company was encouraged to suggest original ideas! He devised a sort of role-playing game where the team considered the subject of the meeting from three points of view: the dreamer (the one with the wildest ideas), the realist (who deals with the practical aspects and the necessary steps), and the critic (who points out any weaknesses or improvements needed). His way of working has become known as the "Disney method," and is used in companies today.

"Of all the things I've done, the most vital has been to coordinate those who worked with me and focus their efforts on the same goal."

PETER PAUL RUBENS

The German artist painted a great many paintings in his career, often in very large formats, yet, he still had time to travel as a diplomat. His secret? Teamwork! He created the compositions of the paintings and painted the people, but everything else—the backgrounds, clothing, and animals— were all painted by his talented assistants.

OTHERS WHO WORKED AS A TEAM

Lise Meitner (1878-1968) The first woman to become a professor of physics in Germany, she led a group of scientists who discovered nuclear fission.

Dorothy Vaughan (1910-2008) A mathematician and computer programmer who became head of computer programming at NASA.

The Beatles (1960-1970) An English rock band formed in Liverpool, regarded as the most influential band of all time.

Howard Carter (1874-1939) A British archaeologist and Egyptologist who discovered the tomb of Tutankhamun with his team in 1922.

ORGANIZE
A BRAINSTORMING SESSION!
You need ideas... lots of ideas!

FIRST FORM A MOTIVATIONAL QUESTION.

Why...?

How...?

What...?

GATHER A GREAT TEAM OF IDEA FINDERS.

Hey, I've got plenty of ideas.

INVITE THEM TO A NICE PLACE.

On the menu today, to inspire you: cooked brain!

Ideally between 4 and 8 people

Don't forget to have drinks and snacks available!

INTRODUCE THE QUESTION AND GIVE THEM THE 'GOLDEN RULES' FOR BRAINSTORMING. YOU CAN ALSO POST THEM ON THE WALL!

BEGIN BY WARMING UP WITH "CREATIVE GYMNASTICS".

"What is red and steals?" (see other ideas on p15 and p35)

THE "GOLDEN RULES" FOR BRAINSTORMING

- The more **IDEAS** the better.
- **WILD IDEAS** are welcome!
- You can **BOUNCE IDEAS** off each other.
- Do not **CRITICIZE ANY IDEAS!**

EVERYONE RECEIVES POST-IT NOTES AND A MARKER TO NOTE DOWN ALL THEIR IDEAS.

139 ideas
138 ideas
137 ideas

PRESENT ALL YOUR IDEAS AND STICK THE POST-IT NOTES ON THE WALL.

I've got a topsy-turvy idea!

AS SOON AS THE GROUP IS OUT OF IDEAS, RE-ENERGIZE THEM WITH AN ACTIVITY FROM THIS BOOK.

I've got an idea! We could...

Great idea! We could also...

WHEN YOU'VE HAD LOTS OF IDEAS AND YOU'RE TIRED OUT, TAKE A BREAK: MOVE, BREATHE, AND RECHARGE YOUR BATTERIES!

Phew... I'm out of ideas.

NOW LOOK AT ALL YOUR IDEAS. ASK EVERYONE TO CHOOSE THEIR 3 FAVORITE IDEAS.

GROUP ALL YOUR CHOSEN IDEAS INTO "EASY," "AMBITIOUS," AND "COMPLETELY WILD."

My idea is great!

Mine too, let's get rich!

WHAT IDEA ARE YOU GOING TO PURSUE NOW, OR LATER? HOW SHOULD YOU GO ABOUT IT?

USE A VARIETY OF TECHNIQUES

like MARCEL DUCHAMP (1887-1968)

Geniuses hate repetition in their work. To nurture new ideas, they don't hesitate to try a variety of techniques or approaches to a problem.

"I forced myself to contradict myself to avoid conforming to my own taste."

It is clear to us, in modern times, that Marcel Duchamp was an artist. But that wasn't so clear to other artists at the time.

In New York in 1917, he exhibited an upturned urinal (calling it *Fountain*) and many scandalized people said "It's not art! Art must be the result of work!" Duchamp liked to push boundaries. His painting *Nude Descending a Staircase* sparked laughter from the art world, and a few years later he created *The Bride Stripped Bare by Her Bachelors, Even*, an oil painting, with paper and lead wire, held between two glass plates. Neither sculpture nor painting, this work of art does not allow itself to be easily defined, just like Duchamp himself.

5 different TECHNIQUES

Imagine that you have a problem and you are looking for a solution. Call on these 5 different people and use them to generate unusual ideas. A variety of people will come up with a variety of techniques for tackling a problem.

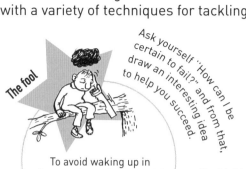

The fool

Ask yourself "How can I be certain to fail?" and from that, draw an interesting idea to help you succeed.

To avoid waking up in the morning, take powerful sleeping pills and put lots of nails on the floor by your bed...

Possible interpretation
Do the opposite and have an energizing fruit juice for breakfast and put a soft rug on the floor by your bed.

Draw a random image and turn it into an original idea.

The fortune teller

The mystic cards have shown me armor! What's an idea that could relate to this?

Battle: the last one down to breakfast gets only dry bread.

Possible interpretation
The last one down for breakfast must clear everything away.

Problem:
You just can't wake up in the morning!

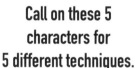

Call on these 5 characters for 5 different techniques.

Imagine that everything is possible: money is no object here.

The magician

You have a magic wand: how could it help you get up in the morning?

I would wake up in a new and interesting place each day. On a beach, in the jungle, in a big city...

Possible interpretation
Download different soundtracks for my alarm clock: waves, birdsong, city sounds, a rainforest storm...

The superhero

What would Leonardo da Vinci do to wake me up?

He'd build a mechanical bed that lifts me into a sitting position when my alarm goes off.

Think of someone you admire and ask yourself how they would solve your problem.

Possible interpretation
Move your alarm clock across the room, so you have to get up to turn it off.

The animal lover

How do animals do it?

I could sleep during the day and be awake at night, like a bat.

Possible interpretation
How about taking a power nap for 15 minutes during the day, to recharge yourself?

KNOW YOURSELF

Like SOCRATES (469-399 BCE)

Real geniuses find roles that combine what they are good at (their talent) and what fascinates them. Some people think the essence of genius is to pursue what makes you happy.

 ### Young geniuses or old masters?

Some people believe there are two types of genius: the "conceptual genius," who experiences a creative explosion when they are young, and does not change much throughout their lives (e.g. Edward Munch, Orson Welles); and the "experimental genius," who arrives at the top later on in life, after much trial and error (e.g. Paul Cézanne, Auguste Rodin).

"People who are asked, provided they are well questioned, find the right answers for themselves."

 Socrates was one of the most famous philosophers of Ancient Greece. His mother was a midwife, and just as she helped women deliver their babies, Socrates helped people give birth to their ideas. When he spoke to prominent thinkers of the day, he made them question whether what they said was true—"I know only one thing; that I know nothing." For Socrates, philosophy allowed everyone to think freely for themselves and not according to the ideas of others. We must therefore get to know ourselves well if we want to become our best and most creative self.

 ## OTHERS WHO KNOW THEMSELVES

Bill Gates (b. 1955) An American computer programmer, entrepreneur, and co-founder of Microsoft Corporation who was excused from math class at school to design early video games.
Coco Chanel (1883-1971) A French fashion designer, businesswoman, and founder of the famous Chanel brand.
Ellen Degeneres (b. 1958) An American comedian, actress, writer, LGBT activist, and the first openly gay actress to play an openly gay character on television.
JK Rowling (b. 1965) A British novelist, screenwriter, and producer, known for writing the best-selling Harry Potter series.

If we don't practice our talents, they can become tired and we can lose them. Why don't you schedule time to practice your talents on your calender?

WHAT'S YOUR GENIUS?

You're brilliant! But the question isn't "how brilliant are you?" (sadly you will probably never match Leonardo da Vinci), but "what are you brilliant at?".

10 TALENTS
First, make a list of everything you're good at. What are your areas of expertise? Name ten of them.

10 PASSIONS
Then make a list of everything you are passionate about. These are areas that interest you and that you want to explore more deeply, even if you are not an expert in the subject!

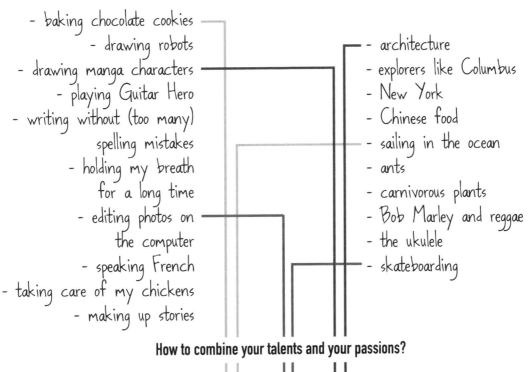

- baking chocolate cookies
- drawing robots
- drawing manga characters
- playing Guitar Hero
- writing without (too many) spelling mistakes
- holding my breath for a long time
- editing photos on the computer
- speaking French
- taking care of my chickens
- making up stories

- architecture
- explorers like Columbus
- New York
- Chinese food
- sailing in the ocean
- ants
- carnivorous plants
- Bob Marley and reggae
- the ukulele
- skateboarding

How to combine your talents and your passions?

Now see in which activities you could use your talents and your passions at the same time.

be a chef on a big yacht

become an architect inspired by Japanese houses

create a fantastic website for skateboarders

"All knowledge is an answer to a question."

GASTON BACHELARD, PHILOSOPHER

"When you drink water,
think of the spring."

CHINESE PROVERB

"Nothing is lost, nothing is created,
everything is transformed."

LAVOISIER, CHEMIST

"He who follows in the footsteps of
the one ahead will never pass him."

MAO TSE TONG, POLITICIAN

TAKE IT FURTHER...

Answers to games and exercises

Short exercises to help you think outside the box (page 40-41)

How many ways can you think of to divide a square into 4 equal parts? Here are a few possible answers. As you can see, it's all about going beyond what we already know!

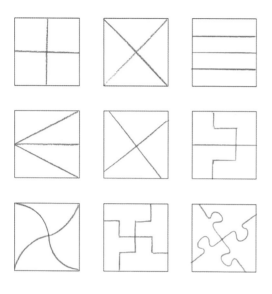

Connect these nine dots using four straight lines.

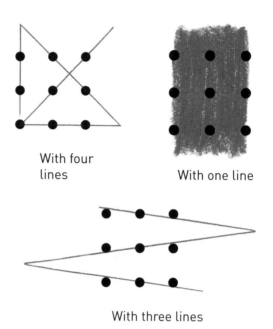

With four lines

With one line

With three lines

Can you rearrange these six matches to make four identical equilateral triangles?

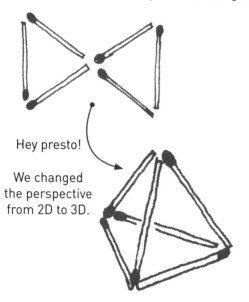

Hey presto!

We changed the perspective from 2D to 3D.

How can you plant ten apple trees in five rows of four?

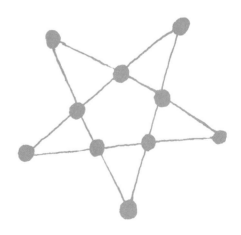

Devious riddles

Can you name three consecutive days without saying Monday, Tuesday, Wednesday, Thursday, Friday, Saturday, or Sunday?
Yesterday, today, and tomorrow.

A police officer sees a truck driver going the wrong way down a one-way street. But she does not stop him. Why?
Because the driver is on foot.

A London hairdresser says he would rather cut the hair of three people from Manchester than one from London. Why?
Because he'd make three times as much money!

There are six eggs in a basket. Six people each take an egg. Why is there an egg still left in the basket?
Because the last person took the basket away with the egg still in it.

Three glasses are filled with juice and three are empty. By moving only one glass, can you organize the glasses so that empty and full glasses alternate?
Pour the juice from the second glass into the fifth glass.

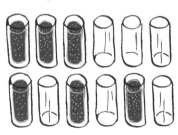

Imagine an extraordinary table
(page 43)

Here are some examples of prototype ideas for a table with no legs, no horizontal surface, or no geometric form...

FURTHER RESOURCES

BOOKS:

- *Mind Maps For Kids: An Introduction*, Tony Buzan (Thorsons, 2003)
- *Invent It*, Rob Beattie (QED Publishing, 2017)
- *Genius: A Photobiography of Albert Einstein*, Marfe Ferguson Delano (National Geographic Kids, 2015)

WEBSITES:

- Agatha Christie: www.christiemystery.co.uk
- Biomimicry: www.asknature.org and www.biomimicry.net
- Biographies of geniuses: www.wikipedia.org
- Napoleon Bonaparte: www.napoleon.org
- Quotes: www.brainyquote.com
- Failures who succeeded: ezinearticles.com/?16-Most-Inspiring-Famous-Failures&id=862208 (16 most inspiring failures by Kenneth Foo)
- Salvador Dali: www.tate.org.uk/kids/explore/who-is/who-salvador-dali

Internet Safey

Children should be supervised when using the internet, particularly when using an unfamiliar website for the first time. Publisher and author cannot be held responsible for the content of the websites referred to in this book.

ACKNOWLEDGEMENTS

Thank you to the careful editors and advisors: Luc de Brabandere, Caroline Devreese, Sophie Hercules, Eric Lardinois, and Mark Raison.
Thanks to Igor Byttebier for the table exercise (p43).

About the author

Philippe Brasseur is a true cultivator of ideas. After careers in advertising, event organization, and children's publishing, he has dedicated himself to creativity and creation since 2000. He is an author, illustrator, and painter, as well as a trainer and consultant in creativity and innovation, for schools, companies, and hospitals. He lives near Brussels with his wife and four children.
Website: www.philippebrasseur.be

YOUR LIFE AS A GENIUS

Everyone can live an exceptional life: a life like no other, where you are fully yourself, and help improve the lives of others. To live that life, the first step is to dare to dream...

What prize or award would you like to win?

Which of your talents would you like to become great at?

Which genius would you love to meet?

What would you like to learn or know how to do?

Your life of curiosity

Your life of determination

How can you positively change the world around you?

Which part of the world would you like to visit most? Why?

YOUR EXTRAORDINARY LIFE

Your life of imagination

What do you dream of creating?

What wild things would you like to do with your life?

What would you like to change or transform?

"In the deepest sense, being creative is to realize oneself as a person."
(Carl Rogers)

AN EXTRAORDINARY WEEK

YOUR *EXTRAORDINARY* LIFE BEGINS TODAY!

Be determined
Write 7 inspiring messages to 7 different people (p56).

Be curious
Draw a self-portrait showing your genius. See how wonderful you are! (p13)

MONDAY

Be imaginative
Say "Hello" in 5 different ways (p35).

Be determined
Mess something up on purpose! (p63)

Be imaginative
Believe that you have superpowers (p37).

TUESDAY

Be curious
Take ten photos of things that touch you or surprise you today (p15).

Be determined
Organize a brainstorming session on a question you're interested in (p65).

Be curious
When you are asked a question, try to answer it with another question (p17).

WEDNESDAY

Be imaginative
Admire a plant for at least 5 minutes (p39).

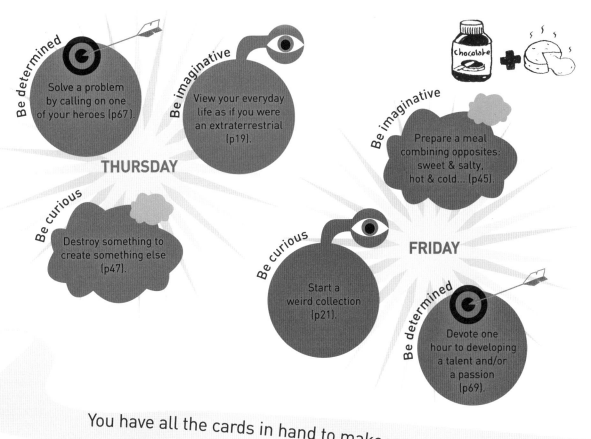

Be determined
Solve a problem by calling on one of your heroes (p67).

Be imaginative
View your everyday life as if you were an extraterrestrial (p19).

THURSDAY

Be curious
Destroy something to create something else (p47).

Be imaginative
Prepare a meal combining opposites: sweet & salty, hot & cold... (p45).

FRIDAY

Be curious
Start a weird collection (p21).

Be determined
Devote one hour to developing a talent and/or a passion (p69).

You have all the cards in hand to make your life a work of art, exciting and unlike any other....

Be imaginative
Go on a trip in a daydream (p51).

Be curious
Talk to someone with a very different talent from yours (p25).

SATURDAY

Be determined
Do something you've been postponing for a long time (p61).

Be determined
Plan your goals for next week, for next year, and for 10 years' time (p60).

SUNDAY

Be curious
Map out all your strengths and qualities (p27).

Be imaginative
Turn your day upside down (p44).

FROM YES, BUT!

After reading this book, you may have lots of plans and ambitions to live an extraordinary life! But when you have big plans, it's perfectly normal to find all sorts of reasons why you can't carry them out: YES, BUT! So here are some ideas to stop the most common causes of—YES, BUT...

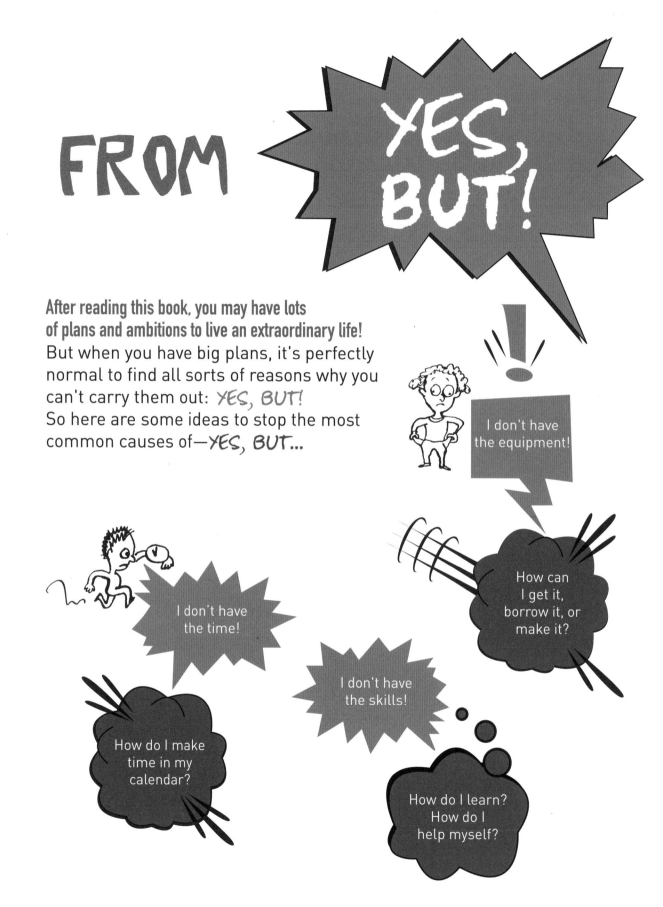

TO **YES!**

I don't have... (whatever is needed)!

How can I do it with what I have on hand?

It's impossible! It's too complicated.

This person doesn't agree!

How do we convince them?

How can I simplify my idea?

It's not working!

It's not important!

What would be the positives if you completed it?

How can I do it better, in another way?

Other people are better than me!

How do I do it my way?